TCHAIKOVSKY

GREAT COMPOSERS

TCHAIKOVSKY

DAVID MOUNTFIELD

CHARTWELL
BOOKS, INC.

This edition published in 1990 by
Chartwell Books, Inc.
a division of Book Sales, Inc.
110 Enterprise Avenue
Secaucus, New Jersey 07094

Prepared by The Hamlyn Publishing Group Limited
a division of The Octopus Publishing Group
Michelin House, 81 Fulham Road, London SW3 6RB

© 1990 The Hamlyn Publishing Group Limited

ISBN 1 55521 6072

Produced by Mandarin Offset

Printed in Hong Kong

CONTENTS

THE
GATHERING
STREAM

Early, often unhappy childhood: Studies and early employment at the conservatoires in St Petersburg and Moscow: first great creative period in the 1870s

Pyotr (Peter) Ilyich Tchaikovsky was born on 7 May (25 April according to the Russian calendar then in use) 1840, into a comfortable middle-class family. His father Ilya was general manager of mines in the industrial centre of Vottkinsk, about 600 miles east of Moscow, a position which made him something like the local squire. His mother Alexandra, who was of French descent, produced six children, Nikolay (born 1838), Pyotr, Alexandra, known as Sasha (born 1842), Ippolit (born 1843), Anatoly and Modest (twins, born 1850). She died of cholera in 1854, aged 41, a

Left *The composer's father, Ilya Petrovich Tchaikovsky, and mother, born Alexandra Assier. She was his father's second wife and her family had a record of neurotic disability which reappeared in her most famous son.*

Right *The Tchaikovsky family. The composer is on the left; the other children are Zinaida (his father's daughter by his first wife), Nikolay, Ippolit (on his father's knee) and, in front, Alexandra (Sasha). The twins Anatoly and Modest (born 1850) had not yet arrived.*

Below *The Tchaikovsky house at Vottkinsk. It is not surprising that a move to the city from this pleasant rural home upset the eight-year-old child.*

Fanny Dürbach. The worst aspect of the move to Moscow was that it entailed the departure of this beloved governess. Tchaikovsky was devoted to his mother, and later to her memory, but there is some evidence that she was less well equipped than Fanny to deal with his difficult temperament.

devastating blow for the 14-year-old Tchaikovsky who never got over it.

Family life was extremely important to Tchaikovsky, and he remained on terms of the closest affection with his siblings, especially Sasha who, in spite of being younger, was something like a second mother to him, and the twins Anatoly and Modest (his biographer), to whom, in turn, he was rather motherly himself.

Another important figure in Tchaikovsky's childhood was Fanny Dürbach, a young woman of Swiss origin who was his governess between the ages of four and eight, possibly the happiest period of his life. It was she who reported on the future composer's early facility for languages and on his ultra-sensitive temperament.

As composers go, Tchaikovsky was a comparatively late developer (certainly by comparison with his hero Mozart), but signs of his obsession were evident then – and worrying to the young governess. One night Fanny came into his room late when he should have been asleep to find him sitting up and overwrought. 'Oh, this music, this music!' he cried. 'It's here,' pointing to his head, 'it won't leave me in peace!' He had already begun piano lessons, and Fanny observed that he was especially nervous

9

after playing the piano or listening to music.

Country life and the companionship of the adored Fanny both ended about the same time, the first great upheaval in Tchaikovsky's life. The family moved to St Petersburg, then the capital of the Russian Empire, in 1848, and Tchaikovsky was sent to a boarding school, where he was insecure, teased and overworked. The result was a breakdown in health and a spell at home under another governess. By 1850 he had recovered and was sent, again as a boarder, to the School of Jurisprudence. When his mother left him there, he clung to her and

had to be pulled away, a scene which made him shudder when he remembered it as a middle-aged man.

He eventually settled down, and he remained at this school, the main purpose of which was to train future civil servants, for nine years. As a student he was better than average but not outstanding. He took lessons in piano and singing, and wrote his first composition (it did not survive) after his mother's death, when music was his only comfort. His first surviving composition dates from 1855: it reveals the influence of his Italian singing master but shows no great

St Petersburg towards the end of the nineteenth century. The family moved here when Tchaikovsky's father's Moscow job fell through, though they did not remain for long.

Above *The House in St Petersburg in which the Tchaikovsky family lived in 1848–9.*

promise and no real originality.

Nevertheless, by this time Tchaikovsky's musical abilities were obvious enough for his father to inquire from his piano teacher, Rudolf Kündinger, a musician of some repute, whether the boy should consider music as a profession. The answer was no, partly because he showed 'no signs of genius' and partly because of the difficulties of earning a living as a musician, no matter how talented.

Accordingly, after graduation in 1859, Tchaikovsky entered the Ministry of Justice as a humble clerk. It was certainly an easier option, since a post in the tsarist civil service was, or could be, something of a sinecure. It was possible to devote a great deal of time to music, or to any other congenial pursuit, while holding such a position. Tchaikovsky himself took leave of absence in 1861 for a three-month tour of European capitals, acting as interpreter for a friend of his father.

As Tchaikovsky's father had recently suffered a severe financial setback, which ruled out any parental allowance, Tchaikovsky for the time being accepted his employment in the Ministry of Justice. He went frequently to the opera, and he began to study harmony in classes subsidised by the Russian Musical Society, an institution founded to promote native musical talent.

THE EMERGENT ARTIST

In 1862 the classes were moved to the Conservatoire of Music, newly founded under the direction of Anton Rubinstein (1830–94), already a famous pianist and composer. Tchaikovsky was drawn into the Conservatoire by degrees, attending first just one class, then two, then

The brothers Anton (left) and Nikolay Rubinstein, founders of the St Petersburg and the Moscow conservatoires respectively, leaders of the 'Western' as opposed to the 'Russian' school of composers, and patrons and friends of Tchaikovsky.

Tchaikovsky's adored sister Alexandra with her husband, Lev Davidov, about 1860.

three. In 1863 he finally gave up his job and became a full-time student, giving piano lessons himself to earn a little money, occasionally performing as an accompanist at concerts, and translating a French book on orchestration. Though able at this time to live with his father, he was, naturally, very short of cash. This, however, was a condition that characterised his existence even when he was internationally famous; it was one aspect of Tchaikovsky's incapacity for dealing with the practical details of everyday life.

He had also begun to compose in earnest. In 1864 Anton Rubinstein asked him to write an overture as a holiday exercise, and Tchaikovsky based it on a recent play by the Russian playwright Ostrovsky, *The Storm*, which he had considered writing as an opera. Rubinstein was not at all pleased with the result, partly because the work required a number of instruments not to be found in the small orchestra that Rubinstein had permitted and partly because the severely classical Rubinstein disapproved of all programme music (i.e. music which tells a story or presents 'scenes'). Nevertheless, *The Storm* offers at least a foretaste of some of Tchaikovsky's finest qualities, notably his dashing orchestration and beautiful melody. There was no performance then, and no performance by Tchaikovsky himself ever, though he did adopt some of the material, according to his economical custom, in later works.

The summer of 1865 Tchaikovsky spent at the home of his sister, Sasha, in Kamenka, not far from Kiev in the Ukraine. She had married Lev Davidov, son of one of the Decembrist revolutionaries of 1825, and for many years their estate became the nearest thing Tchaikovsky had to a home, and their children his closest family.

At Kamenka Tchaikovsky wrote a set of dances which were performed in September at an open-air concert in Pavlovsk conducted by Johann Strauss the Younger. This was the first public performance of a work by Tchaikovsky. Later in the year, at the Conservatoire, some fellow students played a movement of a string quartet and Tchaikovsky himself conducted an overture in F. Both of these works were also composed during the summer holiday at Kamenka.

But Tchaikovsky's days at the St Petersburg Conservatoire were drawing to a close. Nikolay Rubinstein (1835–81), brother of Anton, had been responsible for founding the Moscow branch of the Russian Music Society which by 1865 evolved into the Moscow Conservatoire. At his brother's suggestion, Nikolay offered the post of professor of harmony to Tchaikovsky. The

The Davidovs' house at Kamenka in the Ukraine, where Tchaikovsky spent many happy days (and, later, some rather miserable ones).

job was less grand than it sounds. The mere notion of a professional music academy was novel in Russia and by comparison with the St Petersburg Conservatoire the Moscow version was a poor country cousin. Tchaikovsky's salary was 600 roubles, then equivalent to about £50 sterling, which explains why Nikolay Rubinstein was unable to attract a musician of more substantial reputation than Tchaikovsky to his staff.

Tchaikovsky's father was incensed at the sum offered, muttering darkly about Italian operatic composers who commanded fifty times as much for a single work. Nevertheless, the post confirmed Tchaikovsky's status as a professional musician.

He was less pleased by the prospect of moving to Moscow – the equivalent of moving from London to Manchester – or of living, though rent-free, in Nikolay

Rubinstein's house. In fact, Nikolay was a better mentor for him than Anton. He was a genial soul, only five years older than Tchaikovsky though their relationship made the gap seem wider, and more in sympathy with the new school of Russian music.

In the 19th century the flame of nationalism burned no less fiercely in Russia than in other European countries. Awareness of the general backwardness of Russian society (the serfs were only freed in 1861 and with disappointingly slight practical effects) tended to augment nationalist fervour in the small but important class of educated people including army officers (like the Decembrists), civil servants, intellectuals and artists, who stood between the unreconstructed aristocracy on the one hand and the huge mass of largely illiterate peasants on the other.

The most obvious expression of Russian nationalism came through the creative arts, and perhaps it was even stronger in music than in literature. To the literary giants of the first half of the 19th century – Pushkin, Turgenev, Dostoyevski, etc. – should be added composers such as Glinka and Dargomizhsky, though eventually their ideas and example were to prove more significant than their actual works. Both were closely associated with contemporary

Left *The staff of the Moscow Conservatoire in 1872. Rubinstein (top centre) is flanked by Hubert (left) and Tchaikovsky.*

writers, and both employed folk music, or folk idioms, in their works, including their operas. (These were not very popular with the largely aristocratic, conservative opera audience of St Petersburg, who preferred Italian opera and were as fearful of revolution in music as in politics.)

The direct successors, in some cases protégés, of Glinka and Dargomizhsky were the group known as 'the Five', or sometimes 'the mighty handful'. The leader of these was Balakirev (1837–1910), whose influence and effect as a catalyst (not least on Tchaikovsky) was to be more important than his compositions. The other members of the group were Borodin (1833–87), Cui (1835–1918) whose writings were more significant than his now long-forgotten music, Mussorgsky (1839–81) and Rimsky-Korsakov (1844–1908). All of the Five were born within seven years of Tchaikovsky, and three of them were composers of the first rank.

Tchaikovsky's relationship with the Five was not to be straightforward. He would be close to them in many ways, but not always entirely in sympathy with their aims or methods, nor they with his: the Five never became the Six. As Tchaikovsky himself often protested, no one could be a more patriotic Russian than he, and to us he seems

Right *Alexander Pushkin, the inspiration of so many Russian composers, addresses the Decembrists (upper-class revolutionaries) in 1825. From a drawing by D. Kardovsky, 1925.*

at times a very Russian composer. But musically Tchaikovsky was a truly individual genius, and his interests extended further than those of more narrowly nationalistic musicians who condemned the presence of 'German' or 'French' elements in his work. Moreover, Tchaikovsky's music, even at it most 'Russian', was often not properly understood even by Balakirev and his group. As Stravinsky was to write in a famous letter to *The Times* nearly 30 years after Tchaikovsky's death, 'Tchaikovsky's music, which does not appear specifically Russian to everybody, is often more profoundly Russian than music which has long since been awarded the facile label of Muscovite picturesqueness.'

In spite of his doubts about Moscow, Tchaikovsky flourished in his early years there. Nikolay Rubinstein admired his abil-

ity and, as director of twice-monthly concerts, was in a position to offer him plenty of opportunities. The critic Laroche, an old friend and, with reservations, a great admirer, also joined the staff of the Conservatoire, and Tchaikovsky soon became friendly with the publisher Jurgenson, a man about ten years older than himself, who was to treat him a great deal better than publishers are wont to treat their clients. Among other friends were the pianist and critic Kashkin, and the cellist and conductor, Albrecht, Rubinstein's right-hand man.

Under the convivial Rubinstein's influence, Tchaikovsky gained his taste for heavy drinking, but he never became a victim of alcoholism, like the unfortunate Mussorgsky. Although he was too shy to make friends easily, Tchaikovsky had a great deal of personal charm, as testified by

Left *Glinka, the leading figure of the first generation of the school of Russian nationalist composers, from a portrait by A. Mitterfellner.*

Below *Rimsky-Korsakov, from a portrait by V. Serov. He began his career in the navy and took to music seriously only under the influence of Balakirev.*

Left *Pyotr Jurgenson, who started his Moscow publishing house in 1861 with the help of Nikolay Rubinstein and published many contemporary Russian composers, including Tchaikovsky.*

19

*Nikolay Kashkin
(1855–84), known
as 'Kotick'
(Tom-cat) by
Tchaikovsky, whom
he introduced to
Mme von Meck.*

almost everybody who knew him, including the numerous children, relations or not, to whom in later years he was known as 'Uncle Peter' (Pyotr). Within a short time he was well known and liked in Moscow's musical circles.

Among those captivated by Tchaikovsky's charm was a Belgian soprano, Desirée Artôt. She was not by any means the first young woman he had attracted, but in this case he found himself talking of marriage. There were drawbacks. For instance, Artôt was set on continuing her career, at that time (1868) a more promising one than Tchaikovsky's, and the composer could see himself trailing around Europe's opera houses in her wake. In the end she left the country with nothing decided, and shortly afterwards married a Spanish singer. Tchaikovsky was not particularly distressed.

A greater obstacle to marriage was Tchaikovsky's homosexuality. If he had lived 100 years later, that would probably have been of little significance, but in his time it was a hideous drawback. For one thing he was ill suited to a life of constant dissembling. Worse than that, he was constantly harrowed by self-disgust. For someone condemned to struggle with an emotionally unstable temperament, his sexual orientation was a psychological burden which was hardly tolerable. Tchaikovsky was doomed by nature to a life of great mental suffering. The paradox is, of course, that had this not been so, he would surely not have produced work that has given the rest of humanity so much joy and satisfaction.

At this time Tchaikovsky had probably not fully faced the fact that he was totally homosexual – insofar as any person is totally one thing or the other. He seems to have felt then – and more disastrously nine years later – that marriage might in some way save him from his inverted desires and, apart from the normal pressures of family and friends anxious to see him married off like themselves, the idea of marriage had other attractions for him. He loved domesticity, home and family, and he was in dire need of a wife, not as a sexual partner, but as someone who would mother him.

FIRST MAJOR WORKS

Among Tchaikovsky's compositions in 1866–68 were an overture on the Danish national anthem, an early example of the 'pageant music' which came so easily to him, and a symphonic fantasy, *Fatum* ('Fate', Opus 77), which is worthy of note as an indication of Tchaikovsky's lifelong, obsessional view of life as a struggle of the individual against irremissible forces. More importantly they included his First Symphony (Opus 13) and his first opera, *The Voyevoda* (Opus 3; the word can be roughly translated as 'governor').

Overwork on the symphony produced a nervous breakdown in the summer of 1866, the symptoms including hallucinations and numbness of the limbs, though of course neither the music nor the sleepness nights spent on it were the primary reason for this collapse. The work was virtually finished in

Désirée Artôt (1835–84) in provocative pose. Tchaikovsky 'fell in love' with her probably because it seemed the time to fall in love with someone and she fitted the bill. She had a long and successful career, and her daughter also became a well-known opera singer.

21

September, however, and was shown to Anton Rubinstein in St Petersburg. He insisted on substantial alterations before performance.

Curiously enough, the symphony was written at about the same time as the First Symphony of Borodin and of Rimsky-Korsakov, two of the 'mighty handful', and it has some characteristics in common with both, including the exploitation of Russian folk music and the technique of Schumann. Since Tchaikovsky had not yet met Balakirev and his group, who indeed were suspicious of him as a member of the Conservatoire, this is a sign of common cultural influences rather than individual co-operation. Nevertheless, Tchaikovsky's symphony, which is sometimes called *Winter Dreams*, was not warmly received in St Petersburg. The Moscow audience was more appreciative. Tchaikovsky revised the work eight years later, and it always remained a favourite of his. Though classed as an 'immature' work, it certainly has some fine passages.

The Voyevoda, like his student overture *Groza* ('The Storm'), was based on a work by Ostrovsky, although this was a full-blown opera. Ostrovsky himself promised to provide the libretto, but as Tchaikovsky lost what he sent him, he got no farther than the first scene of Act II and Tchaikovsky himself was forced to complete it. He finished it in the summer of 1868 while in Paris with his great friend and pupil, Vladimir Shilovsky, a rich man who, like his brother Konstantin, owned a large estate where Tchaikovsky was a frequent visitor.

The first performance of *The Voyevoda* took place early in 1869. According to Tchaikovsky it was a 'brilliant success' with the public. But the critics were not so enthusiastic. Especially upsetting was the reaction of his friend Laroche, who complained of the absence of 'any Russian quality' – an extraordinary comment since the opera is packed full with folk-music idioms. Tchaikovsky himself, however, eventually concluded that the opera was a failure, and he burned it, though he salvaged a good deal for use in later works, *Swan Lake* among them. From this experience he

Herman Laroche (1845–1904), a fellow-student of Tchaikovsky at the Moscow Conservatoire and a leading music critic. Despite some professional disagreements, they remained good friends.

Richard Wagner (1813–83). Tchaikovsky, whose judgments were inclined to be subjective (and were especially severe on the successful Romantics), once described Wagner's mighty operas as fatiguing.

learned the lesson that, in opera, what the audience sees is hardly less important than what it hears. 'The composer [of an opera]', he was to write later, 'must constantly think of the stage, i.e. not forget that the theatre needs not only melodies and harmonies but action to hold the attention of the theatregoer.'

By this time Tchaikovsky was fully embarked on what, with hindsight, we can regard as his first great creative period, which lasted until the dreadful personal crisis which overwhelmed him in 1877. His second great period lasted roughly from 1885 to his death.

Not too much should be made of these divisions, however. Although Tchaikovsky was well aware of the importance of artistic inspiration, he was not one of those artists who sits around waiting for inspiration to strike. He was a composer and, he said, the duty of a composer is to *compose*. Except for relatively short periods when rendered incapable by illness, his output was never seriously checked. Even when not truly committed to the work in hand, he could often write at a great rate and with amazingly successful results. Some of his most popular

pieces (e.g. the *1812* Overture) belong to this category. However, this was not his characteristic way of working. Total commitment and intense identification with his subject, to a point at which, as with the First Symphony, his health suffered – these were the marks of Tchaikovsky the composer.

In spite of the only modest success of the First Symphony and the relative failure of *The Voyevoda*, symphony and opera suggested future lines of development. Nor were the two so distinct as might be generally assumed. The narrative means natural to the theatre also touched the music intended for the concert hall. Tchaikovsky believed that music should say something, or at least express a view of life (his own or life in general). Very little of Tchaikovsky's music was 'abstract' or 'absolute' – existing as beautiful sounds but nothing more. The sounds were nonetheless beautiful, as music, Tchaikovsky said, should always be. He once wrote after a surfeit of Wagner (anathema to Tchaikovsky) that 'up to now we tried to charm people by music, now one tortures and exhausts them'.

The period of the 1860s and 1870s was also Tchaikovsky's most nationalistic phase.

The spires of the Kremlin from across the Moscow River. From a print of about 1840.

He met Balakirev and other members of his circle for the first time in 1868, and although there were certain reservations, he received a warm welcome on the whole. When Borodin and Rimsky-Korsakov were in Moscow in 1870 they visited Tchaikovsky every day as a matter of course.

It is in a way paradoxical that Tchaikovsky was based in the historical heart of Muscovy while the high priests of Russian nationalism were in St Petersburg, a city of comparatively recent origin founded with a deliberately Western outlook. The Five were, however, rather more reliable on literary matters than Tchaikovsky, whose literary taste was unpredictable (one reason why the librettos of his operas are in general rather weak). Borodin and Rimsky-Korsakov, on the other hand, had the capacity to write the words and music of

their songs almost as a single creative act.

On the other hand, the St Petersburg group lacked Tchaikovsky's background in musical theory, not that they considered that a disadvantage. Tchaikovsky sometimes complained of their poor composition, while they regarded his harmonies – for instance, in the arrangement of 50 Russian Folk Songs which Jurgenson published in 1869 – as too academic and lacking in inspiration. His overture *Romeo and Juliet*, composed at the same time, had been suggested by Balakirev, and though Balakirev had some extensive criticisms to make of it (Tchaikovsky later revised it accordingly) and the first performance under Nikolay Rubinstein was not a success, Balakirev deserves the credit for instigating what is widely regarded as Tchaikovsky's first indisputable masterpiece. Together with the First String Quartet (Opus 11) of 1871, it marks the coming to maturity of Tchaikovsky's musical genius.

THE
NEED FOR SUCCESS

At least *Romeo and Juliet* was performed. Tchaikovsky's second opera, *Undine*, never reached that stage. It was rejected by the Imperial Theatre in St Petersburg, and when Tchaikovsky got the score back, he destroyed it. Undiscouraged, he was soon at work on his third opera, *The Oprichnik* (royal bodyguard).

Undine was not entirely wasted. As usual, some of the material reappeared later in different forms. The wedding music, for example, appears in the slow movement of the Second Symphony, which Tchaikovsky largely completed while staying at Kamenka with the Davidovs in the summer of 1872. Known as the 'Little Russian' symphony, it included Ukrainian (i.e. 'Little Russian') folk songs, and there is an amusing story concerning the exciting tune which forms the basis of the last movement.

Tchaikovsky was composing, as he normally did, at the piano, and while he was playing this tune, the Davidovs' butler entered the room. 'Excuse me, sir,' he said, 'you have got that wrong.' He then proceeded to sing the 'authentic' version. The butler's rendition, it is said, is faithfully reflected in the variations on the melody which make up the last movement of the symphony.

The cast of a performance of The Oprichnik *by graduates of the St Petersburg Conservatoire. The opera was finished by June 1872 but not produced at the Imperial Theatre until 1874.*

The Second Symphony was performed in Moscow early in 1873 with Nikolay Rubinstein conducting, to warm applause. One of Tchaikovsky's most joyous works, it was also favourably received in St Petersburg, where its nationalistic character went down well with the Five.

By this time Tchaikovsky had already finished his third opera, *The Oprichnik*, which was awaiting the verdict of the committee of the Imperial Theatre in St Petersburg. It was not produced until the spring of 1874, and in the interval Tchaikovsky had produced, among lesser works, his symphonic fantasy on Shakespeare's *The Tempest* (Opus 18), which is a good deal less successful than *Romeo and Juliet*, as well as the Second String Quartet (Opus 22) which 'simply flowed' out of him.

His new status as one of Russia's foremost composers was signified by a commission from the Bolshoi to compose incidental music for Ostrovsky's play *The Snow Maiden*. With the aid of skilful salvage work on *Undine*, it took him three weeks, and he was sufficiently pleased with the result to consider a full-scale opera, but Rimsky-Korsakov beat him to it.

The Oprichnik finally opened in St Petersburg less than three months after Mussorgsky's *Boris Godunov* and, odd though it may seem to us, had rather more success than that great masterpiece, in spite of a shoddy production and an almost complete loss of enthusiasm during rehearsals by the composer, who never regained any liking for the work (he liked *Boris Godunov* even less). Within 48 hours of the final curtain Tchaikovsky was in Venice, a characteristic flight which, however, brought little consolation since Venice was cold and scruffy. He was also feeling guilty about spending so much money on the trip, especially as his brother Modest was at the time in dire financial straits.

EARLY TRAVELS

In these years Tchaikovsky managed to travel extensively (though not as much as he did later) in spite of a constant shortage of cash all the more acute since he had finally acquired his own Moscow apartment. He found some additional income by working as a music critic for several years. The humdrum motive of money was at least one of the reasons for the profusion of his musical output. The First String Quartet, for example, had been composed largely because Tchaikovsky was eager to stage a concert entirely of his own

The Grand Canal in Venice, where Tchaikovsky fled in ill humour after the opening of The Oprichnik *in April 1874.*

works which, he hoped, would raise cash but demanded music for a smaller ensemble than full orchestra. Chamber music never really touched his deepest interests, though he handled it with great facility.

Tchaikovsky's chief summer refuges in Russia were the Davidovs' estate in Kamenka, where he had his own house but ate with the family, and Shilovsky's estate at Ussovo, where he sometimes stayed on his own and, rather sadly, came to prefer solitude to the company of his host, with whom friendship was fading. He would also visit another friend, Nikolay Kondratyev, at Nizy, also in the Ukraine.

In most years of the decade ending in 1877 he managed a trip abroad, usually with friends, or relations, or both. He visited Finland in 1867; Berlin and Paris in 1868; Paris and various German cities (including Mannheim for the Beethoven Centenary) in 1870, making a brief dash into Switzerland

to escape the Franco-Prussian War, and thence to Vienna; Germany, Switzerland and Italy in 1873; Italy in 1874 (after his flight from *The Oprichnik*); Paris, where he was bowled over by Bizet's *Carmen*, Vichy, on doctor's orders, and Bayreuth, where he was bowled over in quite the opposite direction by Wagner's *Ring*, in 1876.

Tchaikovsky's frequent travels suggest a certain restlessness, the compulsive wanderings of a troubled spirit. They did not bring much solace as a rule. Though he was often anxious to get away to 'the West', and eager to get out of Moscow, hardly was he across the Russian frontier before reaction set in. The homesickness often expressed in his letters would be almost comical at times, by comparison with his excited anticipation so shortly before, were it not for our consciousness of the neurotic forces which drove him from place to place. As one of his family remarked, it was not just

Bayreuth Festival Opera House, the famous Wagnerian shrine. Tchaikovsky admitted that 'if Wagner's harmonies are at times open to objection as being too complicated and artificial, and his theories. . . false. . .yet the Nibelungen Ring *is an event of the greatest importance, . . . an epoch-making work'.*

27

Left The Paris Opera, 1875. *According to Tchaikovsky, writing in 1868, standards of production were very high. St Petersburg had 'no idea of such productions', in which the smallest detail rated close attention.*

Tchaikovsky (right) and his brother Modest at San Remo in 1878. With them are little 'Kolya', Modest's deaf-and-dumb pupil, and Alexey Sofronov, the composer's valet.

that he was a wanderer: he was frequently on the move within the same city. He moved from one home to another in Moscow, although by the mid-1870s he felt more at home there than he had ever felt in St Petersburg. And when, rather late in life, he finally acquired a country residence of his own, he inhabited three different houses in the same district within seven years.

For many composers such a peripatetic existence would have had a disastrous effect on creativity. But it seems to have made little difference to Tchaikovsky. There were often distractions, such as English ladies practising the piano in adjacent rooms, but he continued to compose, wherever he was.

A man as inept as Tchaikovsky at managing the ordinary affairs of existence might have been expected to find the inevitable little problems of travel difficult to cope with; but he indulged in one luxury (though it would hardly have been considered that for a middle-class bachelor 100 years ago) – a personal valet. In later years he came to rely heavily on this loyal and devoted servant.

Outside his music, poor Tchaikovsky did commit some fearful errors in life. A minor but curious one was connected with a prize offered by the Grand Duchess Helena Pavlovna for an opera with a libretto based on a story by Gogol. The libretto had been commissioned for the composer Serov, whose sudden death in 1871 left the project without a composer. The deadline set for the

competition was August 1875, but Tchaikovsky somehow got hold of the idea that it was seven months earlier. Accordingly he composed *Vakula the Smith* at breakneck speed, and submitted it in the early autumn of 1874. Only then did he discover that it was a whole year early, whereupon he caused considerable offence by trying to have it withdrawn from the competition and produced at the Imperial Opera. His request was rejected, but now the competition rules had been broken since all entries were supposed to be anonymous. It won anyway, in due course, and was eventually performed in December 1876. Cui, an extremely frosty critic as a rule, reviewed it favourably, but perhaps predictably the public response was cool. Nearly ten years later Tchaikovsky revised the opera as *Cherevichki* (The Slippers), and as late as 1890 he remarked to Jurgenson that he considered it 'almost my best opera'. Though seldom performed now, some critics would tend to agree with the composer's judgment.

THE FIRST PHASE ENDS

Tchaikovsky's first great creative period was approaching a climax. His next major work, composed in 1874, was the First Piano Concerto (Opus

23). This is, without much doubt, the most-loved, most-performed piano concerto ever written (with the possible exception of Beethoven's *Emperor*). Its genesis, however, was none too happy.

Legend says that Tchaikovsky originally meant to dedicate it to Nikolay Rubinstein, though there seems to be no evidence to this effect. At any rate, when Rubinstein heard the work for the first time he strongly objected to it, and according to Tchaikovsky's later account, said so in no uncertain terms, adding that he would not play it in its present form. So hostile was his reaction that Tchaikovsky, always sensitive to criticism, especially from friends, felt deeply insulted, and stalked off swearing he would not alter a single note.

In fairness to both it should be said that some of Rubinstein's criticisms have been made by other critics, that Tchaikovsky did make changes later some of which confirmed the justice of Rubinstein's complaints, and that Rubinstein eventually changed his opinion; he performed the concerto many times in later years.

In the event the dedicatee was the internationally famous pianist Hans von Bülow, who gave the first performance in Boston, Massachusetts, in 1875. The telegram he

Hans von Bülow (1830–94), the pianist and conductor, husband of Liszt's daughter, who later left him for Wagner. He helped popularise Tchaikovsky's music, especially the First Piano Concerto.

sent to Tchaikovsky recounting its enormous (slightly exaggerated) success is traditionally said to have been the first telegram ever sent direct from Boston to Moscow. The first performance in Moscow was given by Tchaikovsky's old pupil and lifelong friend, Sergei Taneyev (1856–1915), and conducted by none other than Nikolay Rubinstein.

In the same year, Tchaikovsky composed his Third ('Polish') Symphony, in which the theme of the struggle against Fate reappears, and began work on *Swan Lake*, commissioned by the Imperial Theatres. In 1876 he wrote his Third String Quartet (Opus 30) and *Francesca da Rimini* (Opus 32), a symphonic fantasia after Dante, which was regarded by Balakirev's group as the best thing that Tchaikovsky had written so far. It owed something to his recent rapturous attendance at Bizet's *Carmen* in Paris and, as Tchaikovsky himself somewhat ruefully admitted, something also to his experience of the *Ring* cycle at Bayreuth during the same trip.

The next year (1877) was Tchaikovsky's year of crisis. In the course of it he wrote two masterpieces (the Fourth Symphony and *Eugene Onegin*), but the composition of those works was intricately bound up with the frightful personal disaster of that year.

Sergei Taneyev (1856–1915), pianist, composer and critic. Tchaikovsky's former pupil and lifetime friend, he gave the first Russian performance of the First Piano Concerto.

Tchaikovsky with his wife,
Antonina Milyukova, at the time
of their wedding in July 1877.

EBB
AND
FLOW

A disastrous marriage and its outcome: Tchaikovsky's relationship with his patroness, Nadezhda von Meck: fame at home and abroad: the country gentleman

Left *Modest Tchaikovsky, from a photograph of 1891. Of all the composer's siblings Modest, though 10 years younger, became the closest to him.*

In 1876 Tchaikovsky announced his intention to get married. To his brother Modest, also homosexual, he wrote that after long consideration he had decided to 'prepare myself for entry into the union of a lawful marriage *with whomsoever I may* [italics added]. I find that our *inclinations* are the greatest and most insuperable obstacle to happiness, and we must with all our strength struggle with our nature.'

Thus did Tchaikovsky attempt to deny his nature by an act of will: a disastrous enterprise.

In 1877 Tchaikovsky was working on his Fourth Symphony, in which his obsession with the idea of Fate (reinforced by his experience of Bizet's *Carmen*) features strongly. He had some problems with it, and his letters testify to a severe bout of depression in the spring, when he also began work on a new opera, *Eugene Onegin*, based on a poem by Pushkin.

He was in a poor state mentally when he received a love letter from a 28-year-old

A production of
Eugene Onegin *by*
the Kirov Opera at
Leningrad in 1987.

woman called Antonina Milyukova, who said she had been a student at the Conservatoire. Tchaikovsky had no recollection of her and he ignored the letter, but she persisted, threatening suicide if he would not meet her. Finally he did meet her. Gently, he discouraged her, but later, returning to *Eugene Onegin*, he was affected by the pathos of Tatyana's unrequited love – also declared by letter – for the hero, and he went to see Antonina again. The upshot was that he proposed marriage, and she accepted smartly.

Antonina was, as Tchaikovsky said, 'not very young' (though nine years younger than he), and she was not very bright. She was also mentally unstable, and was to spend the last 20 years of her life in an asylum. Tchaikovsky appears to have told her that their marriage would have to be platonic, though without explaining exactly why. It would have been surprising if the unfortu-

nate Antonina had taken this seriously: among her delusions she believed that she was overpoweringly attractive sexually.

They were married on 18 July. Of Tchaikovsky's family, only Anatoly was present. Sasha had not been told until the last moment.

In the short interval of his engagement, Tchaikovsky appeared unusually calm. 'What will be, will be,' he wrote in a private letter. What use struggling against Fate? Although the last movement of the Fourth Symphony suggests emotional turmoil not far below the surface, there is no sign of this in *Eugene Onegin*, which he was writing with what was, even for him, extraordinary speed. The music leaves no doubt of his intense involvement with his heroine, Tatyana.

After the wedding the couple set off for St Petersburg to visit Tchaikovsky's old father, whose late and highly successful now that his wife was boring, but the feelings she inspired in him were far stronger than boredom. He was consumed with loathing, fear and despair.

Were the whole story not so sad, one incident would be almost comical. Tramping the Moscow streets for hours at night, Tchaikovsky deliberately waded into the icy river in hope of catching pneumonia. Thus, with luck he thought, death could be brought about without the stigma of suicide. He went home dripping wet and told Antonina he had fallen in accidentally. Physically robust, he did not even catch a cold.

Mentally, however, he was at breaking point. After less than two weeks of cohabitation, he arranged through Anatoly a phony summons to St Petersburg. When Anatoly met him at the station he was shocked at his appearance and took him at once to a hotel. No sooner had they arrived than Tchaikovsky collapsed. He went into a coma from which he did not emerge for two days. The doctor recommended rest and a complete change of environment. In short, the marriage was effectively over.

Spouses cannot, fortunately or not, be disposed of quite so easily. On the whole Antonina, for whom one must feel a good deal of sympathy whatever her motives, was less trouble than she might have been. But trouble she certainly was.

Anatoly, accompanied by Nikolay Rubinstein, informed her of the situation and persuaded her to move to Odessa, a good long distance away but, they vainly hoped, an attractive enough place for her to settle there. She agreed, surprising them by her calmness. Possibly she too felt some relief at the turn of events; but what apparently impressed her most about this occasion was that so great a personage as Rubinstein had taken tea with her.

Antonina did not, however, leave her husband untroubled thereafter. Her occasional letters, and more especially her visits, caused him great distress. At one time she moved into the same building. She also pestered Sasha's family. Feeling sorry for her, Sasha invited her to stay at Kamenka for a time, but eventually had to call upon the long-suffering Anatoly to take her away.

Divorce proved impossible. Antonina agreed to it in theory but was unwilling to accept adultery as the grounds, and adultery was the only feasible cause for which a divorce might have been obtained. She soon provided plenty of evidence for it, with several illegitimate children, but Tchaikovsky naturally feared that his wife, whose

marriage to a simple peasant woman may also have been an influence on Tchaikovsky's conduct. 'When the train started to move,' Tchaikovsky wrote to Anatoly, 'I was ready to scream; sobs choked me. But I had to engage my wife in conversation as far as Klin so as to have the right to lie in the dark in my own armchair, alone with myself. . .' Five days later he told Anatoly that his wife was physically repulsive to him, and little more than a month after that he was off – to the Caucasus, to take a cure. Doctor's orders, he told his possibly sceptical wife.

In fact he fled to Kamenka, to be comforted by Sasha and her family, and to such effect that by the end of August he was able to resume work.

A month later he returned, with profound foreboding, to Moscow, where a new apartment had been made ready and classes were due to begin at the Conservatoire. He wrote

symptoms of mental illness grew stronger as time went on, might say something to damage his reputation.

Yet one effect of his marriage was, rather surprisingly in view of its rapid failure, to stem, temporarily at least, the rumours of Tchaikovsky's homosexuality.

NADEZHDA VON MECK

This disastrous episode was nearly the end of Tchaikovsky. He could hardly have survived it without the loving support of family and friends, nor without his relationship with another woman which had begun shortly before Antonina made her appearance in his life.

Nadezhda von Meck (1831–94) was a wealthy widow. Her husband had come from nowhere to make a large fortune as a railway magnate, largely through his wife's business acumen. Besides this useful talent, she had also accompanied his violin on the piano and had borne him eleven children. (Actually, there were twelve, but the father of the last had been her husband's secretary. According to family legend it was learning of his wife's adultery, through one of their daughters, some four years later that had caused her husband's fatal heart attack.)

In 1876 Mme von Meck approached Nikolay Rubinstein to ask if he could recommend a violinist who would play duets with her. He suggested Iosif Kotek, who was newly graduated from the Conservatoire and short of money. A strong attachment existed between Kotek and his former professor of harmony – Tchaikovsky – and it was no doubt at Kotek's instigation that Mme von Meck wrote to Tchaikovsky to ask if he would provide (for a fat fee) some arrangements of his music for violin and piano. Tchaikovsky did so quite promptly, and Mme von Meck sent a formal though fulsome note of thanks, signing it with 'my sincerest respect and sincerest devotion', which moved the composer to a brief, conventionally grateful response. Thus began, in the words of Tchaikovsky's recent biographer (David Brown), 'one of the most famed and extraordinary correspondences in the whole history of Western culture.'

With Mme von Meck Tchaikovsky enjoyed the closest emotional involvement of his life, at least with any person other than the two or three members of his family who were closest to him. Their enormous correspondence ('this heaving mass of epistolary prose' as David Brown calls it) tells more about Tchaikovsky, more about his attitude to composing and to life in

Nadezhda von Meck (1831–94), a strange and fascinating woman with whom Tchaikovsky conducted an extraordinary correspondence for many years. Although they never met, she became the most important person in his life.

general, than any other source. Though he did not tell her everything, and his letters, like all such letters, were to some extent tailored to his conception of his correspondent, there were some things he would confide to her that he would not tell any other person. Among them were his sharply hostile comments on people like Nikolay Rubinstein who otherwise appear as his closest friends, and on Balakirev and his group, now past their peak and of decreasing interest to Tchaikovsky.

Naturally these remarkable correspondents, who discussed every conceivable subject, from religion to the weather, had much in common. Both were solitary indi-

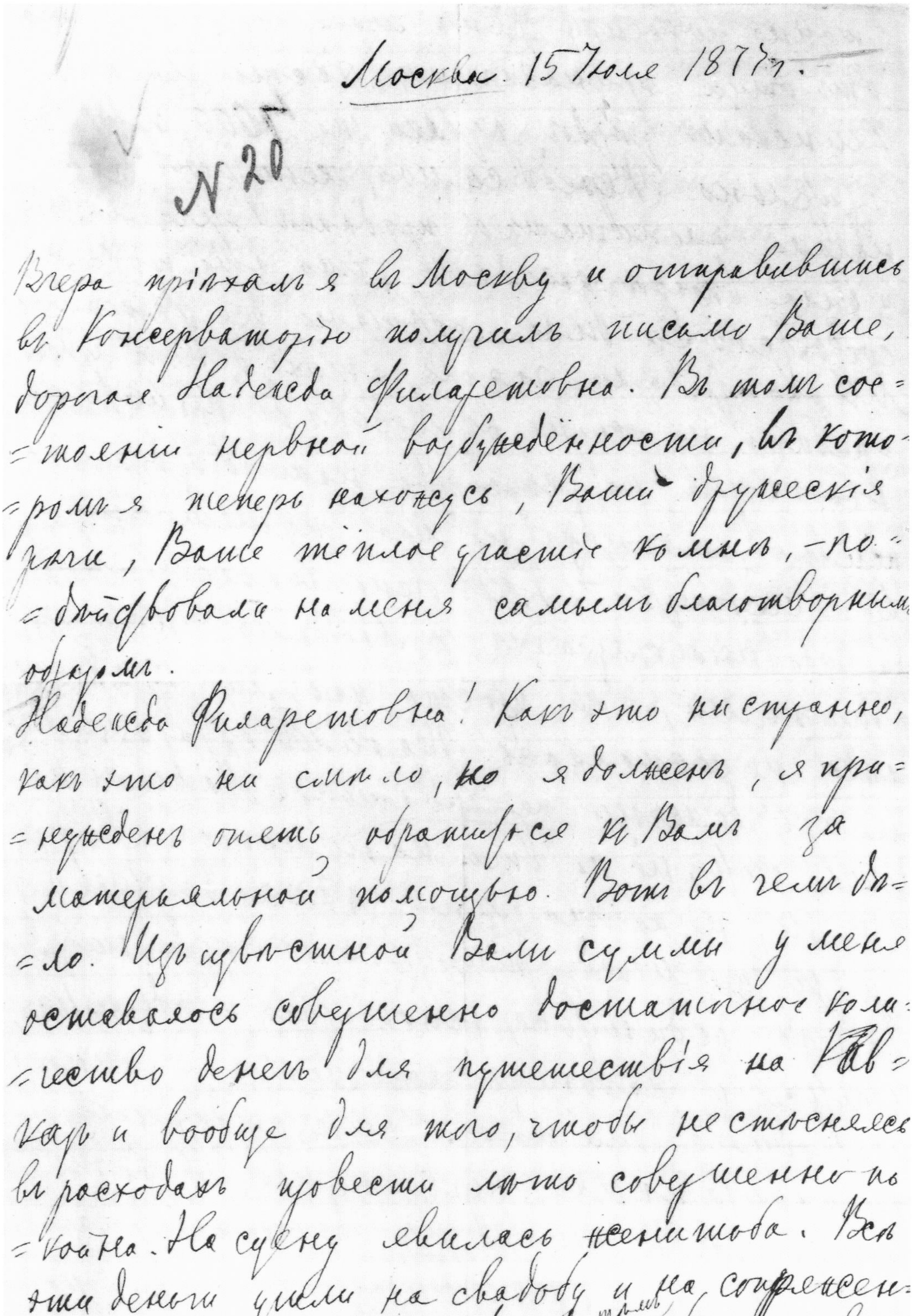

Москва. 15 Июля 1877 г.

№ 25

[handwritten letter in Russian cursive]

A page of a letter from Tchaikovsky to Mme von Meck written nine days after his marriage, expressing gratitude for her sympathy (she wisely concealed her intense resentment of his marriage) and requesting cash in order to take a cure in the Caucasus. She sent 1,000 roubles, but instead of going to the Caucasus, he visited the Davidovs at Kamenka.

viduals, partly by nature, partly by circumstance, the result of temperaments which were forever seeking, yearning, hoping, despairing – never content.

Mme von Meck, moreover, was some nine years older than Tchaikovsky, and was something of the mother-substitute he needed. Yet not one in any obvious sense because, for all their intense involvement with, their delight in, and their admiration for each other, these two troubled, attractive people *never met*.

This was by mutual agreement. There were occasions, in the concert hall for example, when both were in the same place at the same time, but they did not acknowledge each other. No doubt they were both afraid that actual acquaintance might spoil things (Tchaikovsky's hero-worship of Tolstoy faltered a bit after he had met the great man), though Mme von Meck's exclusiveness went neurotically far (she saw almost no one but family and servants, travelling by private train). Yet sometimes proximity existed by design. In 1878 they deliberately planned to be in Florence at the same time, and not far apart: Mme von Meck was seen to pass by Tchaikovsky's windows. This was their 'honeymoon'. Tchaikovsky sometimes stayed in a house on her estate when she was in residence. She informed him of the times she would be taking her walks so that he could avoid her, but on one famous occasion he or she made a mistake and they came face to face in the woods. She appeared dismayed. Tchaikovsky lifted his hat, bowed, and passed on without a word.

Mme von Meck provided much more than emotional support and friendship: she also provided cash, and plenty of it. Beginning with generously rewarded commissions, progressing to loans (requested by Tchaikovsky at the time of his marital crisis), this strange and generous lady then offered to make him an annual allowance of 6,000 roubles, which she continued to pay for 13 years.

Tchaikovsky's finances always remained shaky, partly because of his own acts of generosity (as late as 1885 he was almost reduced to pawning his watch), but from this time onward he had no real reason to feel financially insecure.

Left The Brailov estate of Mme von Meck. Tchaikovsky stayed in the main house when the owner was absent, otherwise in an old cottage on the estate in the village of Simaki, surrounded by 'ancient oaks and limes'.

EQUILIBRIUM REGAINED

After his breakdown, Nikolay Rubinstein awarded Tchaikovsky a sabbatical year (with pay), and he spent an extended vacation abroad, mainly at Clarens in Switzerland with Anatoly. He had long grown bored with teaching. 'For ten years I taught harmony, and during that time I hated my classes, my pupils, my text book and myself as a teacher', he told

A view of Lake Geneva. Tchaikovsky spent a long vacation at Clarens, overlooking the lake near Montreux, in 1878.

Rimsky-Korsakov, no doubt with some exaggeration. When he returned to Moscow in September 1878, he was able, thanks to Mme von Meck's patronage, to resign his professorship.

This in turn freed him to indulge his nomadic urges. Henceforth he was seldom in one place, or one country, for more than a few months at a time.

Both the Fourth Symphony and *Eugene Onegin*, possibly Tchaikovsky's finest works so far, were completed in 1878. While in Switzerland he also wrote the Violin Concerto (Opus 35) and the Piano Sonata (Opus 37).

The Fourth Symphony was dedicated to Nadezhda von Meck. Although its most emotional, almost hysterical passages perhaps owe more to the other woman who so influenced his destiny at this period, his relationship with Mme von Meck is the more important. Tchaikovsky was very happy with the work, which had occupied him a long time. It was first performed, conducted by Nikolay Rubinstein, less than two months after the last note was written early in 1878. Tchaikovsky's friends were less than enthusiastic. Taneyev, one of the composer's most loyal friends and supporters, complained of too much 'ballet music' and said he had the impression it was 'programme music'. Tchaikovsky did not disagree, but he saw nothing wrong with either characteristic in a symphony. Nevertheless, the 'programme', as he explained it with his usual clarity and conviction to Mme von Meck, seems to bear little relationship to the actual music at many points.

Whatever the autobiographical authenticity of the Fourth Symphony, it represented a distinct step forward technically. The first movement in particular is the most daring symphonic movement Tchaikovsky had yet composed, though the finale is less successful than the finale of the Second Symphony.

Eugene Onegin was not performed until 1879. Generally regarded as the greatest of Tchaikovsky's operas, it was unusual (as the composer recognised) in that it lacked powerful dramatic action. 'Maybe my opera won't be theatrical,' he mused, though posterity might argue, looking at his operatic output as a whole, that this was not such a drawback as he feared. The work was so deeply personal, however, that Tchaikovsky was not too concerned about its commercial prospects. He was not keen on giving it to the Imperial Theatres, with their conventional routines, big stars more interested in their own reputations than the music, and mediocre directors, and eventually the first performance was given by the students of the Moscow Conservatoire. The composer received a warm welcome, but Tchaikovsky felt that the applause was for him personally rather than for the opera. He left town by the mail train.

However, the critics praised the opera: Tchaikovsky's forebodings proved chimerical. Two years later it was performed at the Bolshoi, and it soon became the Russians' favourite national opera, along with Glinka's *A Life for the Tsar*. When Alexander III went to a performance, he invited the composer to the royal box, and

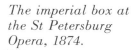

The imperial box at the St Petersburg Opera, 1874.

the opera has remained in the international repertoire ever since.

Tchaikovsky's solitary Violin Concerto was a product of the burst of creativity he experienced in Switzerland when he was emerging from the shadows of his marriage. The immediate cause was the arrival at his villa by Lake Geneva of Kotek, Mme von Meck's protégé and Tchaikovsky's beloved ex-pupil (any sexual attraction was probably one-sided, as Kotek was a great one for the ladies). Notwithstanding the Russian melancholy of the second movement, the Violin Concerto is one of Tchaikovsky's most joyful works, but in spite of the help given by Kotek, the work was dedicated to another violinist and first performed by yet a third. The critic Hanslick wrote a notorious review in which he remarked that the music 'stank' (Tchaikovsky could repeat the whole vicious article from memory years later), but after a mixed reception at first, the concerto became very popular and, combining beautiful melody with ample opportunity for virtuoso soloists to display their technique, it has remained so. Tchaikovsky, at the time reading Dickens's *Bleak House*, was especially pleased by the success of the first performance in England.

The Piano Sonata was begun shortly before the Violin Concerto and laid aside on Kotek's arrival at Clarens. The two works offer an interesting contrast. None of the inspiration of the latter work is apparent in the sonata, probably because there was no equivalent of Kotek to act as a catalyst.

The creative outburst of which the Violin Concerto was the peak marks the beginning of a fallow period in the composer's life. During the next seven years he wrote no great masterpiece. He was not idle, always believing that a composer should compose just as a plumber should plumb (inspiration did not visit the lazy, he said) and seldom completely bereft of ideas for long, but except for the productive year of 1880 his output was much less and major works were rare and undistinguished.

While he was staying at Mme von Meck's estate of Brailov (during her absence) in 1878 he wrote his pieces for children known as the *Children's Album*. They were dedicated to his nephew Vladimir Davidov, known as 'Bobyk' or 'Bob'. Then only seven years old, Bob was to play an increasingly important part in Tchaikovsky's life, as the last of the young men with whom he formed a powerful bond based on sexual attraction.

Later that year he returned to Clarens, a place of which he had grown very fond since he fled there with Anatoly after his marital

fiasco. There he worked on his opera *The Maid of Orleans*. He had long been fascinated by Joan of Arc, but the opera, first produced in St Petersburg in 1881, hardly does justice to his enthusiasm for its subject.

A much more successful work was the *Italian Capriccio* (Opus 45) of 1880, which originated in his desire while in Rome to write something in the manner of the Spanish overtures of Glinka. The joyfulness of the Violin Concerto is here again evident, and Tchaikovsky's confidence was justified when he wrote at an early stage of composition, 'I think I can predict a good future for it'. Moscow went wild over it, as it did not long afterwards over the Serenade for String Orchestra (Opus 48).

Vladimir ('Bob') Davidov, Tchaikovsky's favourite nephew, to whom he wished to dedicate his last great symphony.

FAME AT HOME AND ABROAD

At about the same time as the delicate and graceful Serenade for Strings, Tchaikovsky was writing another piece of strikingly different character. Nikolay Rubinstein had been appointed head of the music section in connection with an exhibition of industry and the arts planned for 1881, and he had commissioned from Tchaikovsky an overture which would open the exhibition. Tchaikovsky was reluctant: it was not the kind of job that attracted him, but he could hardly refuse Rubinstein's personal request. After prolonged delay he got down to work on it at last in October, 1880, and finished it, apart from the orchestration, in less than a week. This was the *1812* Overture, nowadays one of Tchaikovsky's most popular works.

No serious critic has ever wasted much time on this overture, nor did the composer cherish any illusions of its true worth. 'The overture,' he told Mme von Meck, 'will be very loud and noisy [it includes peals of bells and cannon fire]. I wrote it without much warmth and therefore there will probably be no artistic merit in it.'

By this time, of course, Tchaikovsky's music was famous internationally. This did not entirely please him: he was gratified to be famous (and admired), but irked by the demands this put upon his retiring disposition.

Though he was still often troubled by lack of money, and on at least one occasion had to ask Mme von Meck to make him an advance on the next instalment of his annuity, his income was increasing as his music was played all round the world. He had been fortunate in having the conductors of both the New York Philharmonic and the New York Symphony (respectively Karl Bergmann and Walter Damrosch) among his earliest admirers abroad. Von Bülow had done wonders with the First Piano Concerto, giving the first English as well as the first American performance. Tchaikovsky was well known in London, Berlin, Budapest and Paris where, though the Fourth Symphony had been hissed, works such as the Third Quartet (Opus 30) were very popular. He sometimes complained of being treated better abroad than he was in Russia, especially in St Petersburg, for he had become a thorough Muscovite and his letters frequently include denigratory remarks about

Tsar Alexander II (reigned 1855–81) in 1877. His great achievement was the emancipation of the serfs, which had daunted earlier emperors, but his moderate liberalism did not save him from an assassin's bomb.

Right *The Winter Palace (now largely the Hermitage Museum), St Petersburg, the backdrop to a powerful scene in* The Queen of Spades.

the (then) capital. In Russia, among other problems, enforced alterations or even cancelled performances sometimes resulted from the censorship, which tended to grow especially tight whenever someone took a shot at the tsar (Alexander II was in fact assassinated in 1881). Tchaikovsky was no politician, but, as his music proclaims, he believed passionately in the freedom of the individual.

His music was of course widely played and appreciated in Russia, not least, in the case of his songs and minor pieces, by amateur musicians, and the importance of his contribution to Russian culture was becoming generally recognised. He enjoyed imperial favour – some of his church music resulted from a suggestion (tantamount to an order) from the tsar – and he numbered the Grand Duke Konstantin Nikolayevich (brother of the tsar) and people like Prince Golitsin among his friends.

Not very close friends, obviously. But even those who appear to have been close friends of Tchaikovsky turn out, on the evidence of his letters, to have been less firmly fixed in his affections than appearances suggested. It is, however, perhaps unfair to place too much weight on a person's private correspondence. Tchaikovsky was anything but malicious, and was sometimes shocked by cruel gossip even

Above Tsar *Alexander III (reigned 1881–94), whose coronation in Moscow (1883) was celebrated with extraordinary magnificence. Tchaikovsky contributed a* Coronation March.

43

within his own family circle.

But the circle of people with whom Tchaikovsky was deeply concerned was a small one – Mme von Meck, Sasha, the twins Anatoly and Modest, a few others like Kotek or Taneyev at certain periods, and not least his valet, Alexey ('Aleysha') Sofronov.

Sofronov was nearly 20 years younger than his master and had succeeded his elder brother in the job. From the first he was as much a companion as a servant, accompanying Tchaikovsky on country walks, sharing his meals, and even going to the theatre with him (in spite of a drastic difference in taste). But he was also a great help and support without whom Tchaikovsky's 'wanderings' would have been much more of a strain. Alexey represented security, and Tchaikovsky was quite depressed at the prospect of his leaving to do military service, though he was able to use his influence to have Alexey's service reduced from the draconian six years nominally required to three. It is right to say that Tchaikovsky loved this young man (among many others) but wrong to suggest that the relationship was physical.

Alexei Sofronov and his wife. He was the devoted servant who relieved Tchaikovsky of the task (for which the composer was ill equipped) of dealing with mundane problems of living.

Nikolay Rubinstein was one of those of whom Tchaikovsky seems to have been less fond than might be expected from the facts of their association. Nevertheless, the sudden death of Rubinstein, who had done so much for his career, in 1881, shortly before he was to perform the premiere of the Second Piano Concerto (Opus 44) which Tchaikovsky had dedicated to him, did upset the composer.

Tchaikovsky was urged to succeed his old friend and mentor as director of the Moscow Conservatoire, but the post did not appeal to him, though he dithered a while before turning it down. Balakirev, who had returned to the musical scene after a nervous breakdown and several years as an official of the railways, also rejected it. Taneyev was Tchaikovsky's choice, but the job was given to Nikolay Herbert, once a fellow-student of Tchaikovsky's in St Petersburg, though not a man he held in much esteem. In fact Herbert soon resigned, and Taneyev then replaced him.

Tchaikovsky wrote a Piano Trio (Opus 50) in two movements in Rubinstein's memory, possibly having in mind a request from Mme von Meck for such a work some time previously. His heart was not wholly in it and the emotion it generates can seem superficial; but it stands out among his compositions of this period.

In the early 1880s Tchaikovsky's relative inactivity as a composer was disguised by the arrival on stage or concert platform of works written earlier, and by a succession of minor compositions and arrangements, by himself and by others, of his works. For instance, the young Debussy (1863–1918), another protégé of Mme von Meck, was responsible for arranging dances from *Swan Lake* as a piano duet.

Tchaikovsky himself, at Kamenka in the summer of 1881, was editing the church music of Bortnyansky (1751–1825), director of the Imperial church choir in the time of Catherine the Great. Undertaken at the request of Jurgenson, it was a considerable labour – the edition runs to ten volumes – but it was not a labour of love. Tchaikovsky said he could not bear Bortnyansky's music. For the moment, though, he had nothing better to do.

The impending coronation of the new tsar (Alexander III) brought another commission. At the – delayed – opening of the international exhibition of arts and industry, a Tchaikovsky concert was given, which included the first performance, by Taneyev, of the Second Piano Concerto (not a great success) and the popular *1812* Overture. At

the concert Tchaikovsky was cheered loudly, confirming his status as Russia's outstanding national composer, and he was commissioned to write a celebratory march for the coronation – the *Moscow* Cantata of 1883. His reward for this was a diamond ring worth 1,500 roubles. He would rather have had the money, especially as, having pawned the ring for 375 roubles, he proceeded to lose both the cash and the pawn ticket.

In November 1881 Tchaikovsky attended the wedding of his niece Vera (Davidova) to Rimsky-Korsakov, an occasion for more gloomy exchanges with Modest on their unhappy fate of being denied the full experience of love. Another marriage which gave him great pleasure was that of Vera's sister, Anna, to Mme von Meck's son, Nikolay, in 1884. In a weird way this was a kind of proxy wedding symbolising the union of Tchaikovsky and Nadezhda von Meck, both of whom had been eager for the match. Mme von Meck, however, did not put in an appearance at the wedding.

The happy home at Kamenka was unfortunately breaking up. Sasha's health had been deteriorating for some time and, taking morphine for relief, she had become addicted to it. Her husband, with financial worries too, was depressed, and her daughter Tanya, after some messy emotional problems, had taken to drink and drugs (she died in 1887). The whole situation had become so gloomy that Tchaikovsky, resorting to a device he had employed before, arranged for Jurgenson to summon him to Moscow on some invented pretext.

Later that year Brailov was sold, and Tchaikovsky feared that Mme von Meck would not be able to continue his stipend. This proved a false alarm: her fortune had been dented but not seriously depleted, and the monthly allowance continued. But Tchaikovsky's country retreats were shrinking, and this must have encouraged him to take the long-delayed decision to acquire a country home of his own.

The composer was in poor shape early in 1884, and the strain of the double production, in Moscow and St Petersburg, of his new opera *Mazeppa* sent him scurrying off to Berlin after the opening night in Moscow, in spite of the fact that the first performance of his Second Orchestral Suite (Opus 53) was due the following evening. He also missed the opening of *Mazeppa* in St Petersburg, where the tsar, who was present, expressed surprise that the composer was not. Nevertheless, shortly afterwards Tchaikovsky was awarded the Order of St Vladimir, fourth class. Modest, anxious about his brother's health, sent an exaggerated account of the

The Davidos and their children, Tchaikovsky's substitute family.

45

opera's success; in fact it was a relative failure.

With Alexey away on military service, Tchaikovsky did not know what to do with himself. He went to Paris for a few weeks, then made his way back to Russia in time for his investiture by the tsar, an event which threw him into a blue funk, though in the event the audience went very well.

COUNTRY RETREAT

One great compensation was Alexey's release from military service, a *sine qua non* when it came to finding a suitable country house. During the summer of 1884 Tchaikovsky was rather busy, not only with his music but also with the misfortunes of other people, such as his old friend Laroche, in declining health, and Kotek, dying of tuberculosis, as well as relations like Modest, who was having trouble with his new play.

In the autumn he was abroad again, but at the beginning of 1885 he advertised in the Moscow papers to rent a *dacha*.

After one unsatisfactory effort, house-hunting rapidly lost its appeal, and in the end he sent Alexey off on his own to rent a house which sounded as if it might be suitable. It was near Klin and, being close to

A Russian family relaxing in the grounds of their dacha. *Tchaikovsky could never settle in any place for long, but on the whole he was happiest in his less stressful rural retreat.*

the railway station, handy for both Moscow and St Petersburg while being sufficiently isolated to ensure seclusion.

When Tchaikovsky saw the house himself, he was disillusioned, but he agreed it would do for a year, and in a short time, notwithstanding unattractive furniture and mice in the dining room, he grew to like it better. 'The lovely view out of the window, the peace and quiet, the feeling that I am in my own home, make me happy,' he wrote to Modest, and 'I have been in a good humour all day.' Alexey had arranged everything, or nearly everything, very well. The bedroom was not satisfactory but 'as I am not good in making things comfortable I do not quite know how to improve [it].'

His work was going well and he was reading a lot, including Dickens – in English, not in Russian translation as previously – and Byron, with whom he was about to become professionally involved. He was able to go to Moscow just for a day, in theory at any rate; more often events conspired to keep him longer in the city. But by the following September he was writing to Modest from Klin that 'I have grown so used to my environment that it seems to me I have always lived here.'

When left to his own devices, Tchaikovsky generally followed a regular routine. At Klin, where he had few visitors (he even

Left *A view of the little town of Klin in the 1890s.*

Below *A pathway in the garden of the Tchaikovsky Museum at Klin.*

cancelled an invitation to Modest in order to get on with his work), he was able to live the peaceful, orderly life he liked. Most of his work was done in the morning, after breakfast. If he were not actually composing, he would be correcting proofs, writing letters or reading. In the afternoon he took a long walk, something he tried to do not only at Klin but wherever he was living. It was during these walks that his mind worked most creatively, when solutions to problems or ideas for future compositions came to him. Sometimes, if he had forgotten his notebook, he would hurry back in order to put something down on paper while it was fresh, though his musical memory was so retentive that this can seldom have been really necessary. In the evenings he worked again from five to seven, read, played the piano, or occasionally cards. His landlady, formerly a rich woman but now living on the rent from the *dacha*, was anxious to engage him in picquet, which he said he could not play. He did call on her occasionally, out of kindness. Since his own feelings were hurt so easily, Tchaikovsky was always, or nearly always, anxious to avoid hurting other people's.

His seclusion led some people to bestow on him the nickname, 'the hermit of Klin', but, as with his landlady, he did not shirk tasks that he considered fell within the realm of social duty. For example, he provided the money to set up a local school in 1886, and continued to subsidise it until his death. Once he even sat in on the lessons.

Even if he had wanted to, Tchaikovsky could not have remained in permanent seclusion in the country. He was now too great a person for that, and he was shortly to become much more of a public figure, and on an international scale, than he would have believed himself capable a few years before. Moreover, even before he took the house at Klin, the mysterious force of artistic inspiration was moving strongly within him once more. The comparatively quiet period in his creative life which had lasted, though not quite unbroken, since 1878, was over, and he was about to embark on the second great period of masterly composition.

HIGH TIDE

International tours as a conductor: a final surge of creativity in ballet, opera and symphonic works: the break with Nadezhda von Meck: last days

T he year in which he acquired his first true home was significant for Tchaikovsky in other ways. Most important, it was the year in which his creative powers were renewed, and he embarked upon a great flood of composition which ran almost unchecked until his death.

The work that released the springs of inspiration was the *Manfred* Symphony, based on the drama by Byron. It is interesting that it was proposed to him as a subject by Balakirev, who was also responsible for initiating the work (*Romeo and Juliet*) that marked the beginning of Tchaikovsky's first great creative period.

Tchaikovsky was not keen on the idea at first. For one thing, Byron's tale had already been the subject of the well-known overture by Schumann, and when he did begin work on it he did so only (he said) because Balakirev would give him no peace otherwise. In his current revision of *Vakula the Smith*, re-named *Cherevichki* (usually translated as 'The Slippers' although the footwear concerned are actually high-heeled boots), Tchaikovsky inserted the Schoolmaster's Song, which has been interpreted as a satirical stab at the didactic Balakirev.

Balakirev even provided the 'programme' for *Manfred* and, once he became engrossed in the work, Tchaikovsky soon felt a sense of identification with his tragic hero: 'at times I myself became Manfred', he told Mme von Meck.

In spite of Balakirev's urging him to take his time, Tchaikovsky wrote *Manfred* very quickly, completing it in September 1885. He told Jurgenson, 'it seems to me that it is the best of my compositions.' He made similar remarks about several of his major compositions, only (as in this case) to change his opinion radically a short time later. Balakirev, however, agreed with Tchaikovsky's initial judgment, and so do many contemporary critics. *Manfred*, which contains many Balakirevian elements of course, has even been favourably compared with Tchaikovsky's next symphony, the Fifth.

Tchaikovsky had put aside his opera *Charodeyka* ('The Sorceress') but took it up again immediately on finishing *Manfred*. The contrast illustrates the importance of emotional commitment on the composer's part. *The Sorceress* was a pot-boiler, a bald attempt to please the public; it was and is generally regarded as a complete failure.

When *Cherevichki* went into rehearsal towards the end of 1886, Tchaikovsky was persuaded to conduct. He had done little conducting since his early days and the fact bothered him, partly because he felt he could get better performances of his music if he did. But the prospect appalled him. 'The nearer the dreaded time,' he wrote to Mod-

In his fifties, Tchaikovsky was beginning to look much older than his years.

est, 'the more I suffered, and many times I wanted to refuse. But in the end – with great difficulty – I forced myself to go.'

The players greeted him enthusiastically, and all went well when he conducted the first performance, following that by conducting *Charodeyka* as well. Critics like Cui praised his conducting. He had overcome this particular neurosis at least.

A NEW CAREER

On the day he first took up the baton again he said that it marked a most significant event in his life. And so it did. For he now embarked on virtually a new career, making a succession of international tours as a conductor. Already a popular composer world-wide, he became a great public figure on the international musical scene. Few musicians before him had enjoyed such wide acclaim at such a compara-

tively young age (47). Moreover, the decisive fact so far as Tchaikovsky was personally concerned, these tours were lucrative.

Tchaikovsky's international standing stemmed, of course, from the popularity of his music, but as with all artists of great stature in their own time, other influences, not least political ones, were at work. In some places Tchaikovsky was seen as an apostle of freedom. Russian society at this time resembled an over-filled kettle coming to the boil; the lid would not stay on much longer. There is nothing much to encourage revolutionaries in Tchaikovsky's music, but he appeared to some – inside and outside Russia – as a manifestation of the aspirations of the Russian people. There were few greater artistic spokesmen for those popular 19th-century creeds, nationalism and liberalism.

The tremendous welcome he received in Prague was partly due to the Czechs' view of him as a leader of Slavic culture, at a time

Left *Tolstoy, one of Tchaikovsky's heroes, from a portrait of 1887. After their meeting Tolstoy sent Tchaikovsky some Russian folksongs to arrange.*

Below *Hauling a barge on the Volga. These men look rather different from the romantically vigorous image of them presented in the 'Song of the Volga Boatmen'.*

Right *The Leipzig Gewandhaus (1845), where Tchaikovsky made his debut as an international conductor while on tour in 1888.*

Below *The old Hamburg Concert Hall, founded by a local merchant, Karl Laeisz, where Tchaikovsky conducted a concert on his second tour in 1889.*

when they were increasingly restive at Austrian rule and inclined to identify with their fellow-Slavs in Russia. In Berlin he was regarded as highly promising but insufficiently Germanic. The chairman of the Hamburg Philharmonic Society commiserated with him for having the bad luck to be born in such a backward country as Russia and suggested he should settle in Germany, where he would soon become a good German composer. In Paris, on the other hand, Germanic influences in Tchaikovsky's work were deplored. The warmth of the reception of new Tchaikovsky works bore a direct relationship to the degree of French influence that Parisian critics detected in them.

In Britain and America judgments tended to be more objectively musical. Some found Tchaikovsky rather too exotic for them; they considered his exciting orchestration and fondness for percussion (with which he achieved novel effects, in advance of his time) rather inelegant. On the whole, though, he was extremely popular with English-speaking audiences: the music was exotic, exciting, yet not too far removed

Above *The Royal Opera House, Berlin, where Tchaikovsky's music was well received by the critics.*

Below *Tchaikovsky with the young pianist Alexander Ziloti (1863–1945), one of many young musicians to whom* *he became attached in his later years. Ziloti advised him on certain changes in the third edition of the First Piano Concerto (1889).*

As an international conductor, Tchaikovsky became acquainted with many notable European composers and performers. He met Brahms in Leipzig on New Year's Day 1888 and liked him, though his comments on his music were sometimes less favourable.

from the comfortingly familiar classical tradition.

Tchaikovsky's first conducting tour began in Germany. In Leipzig he had his famous meeting with Brahms, whom he described without malice as a fat, red-faced little man who drank too much, and with Grieg. He got on well with both of them, although he and Brahms had rather scant admiration for each other's music. Among other musicians he encountered was the young pianist Alexander Ziloti (1863–1945), who became a great support to him, and, in Prague, Dvořák, whom he liked very much (Dvořák ingratiated himself by expressing great admiration for Tchaikovsky).

Arriving in England after a Channel crossing that had filled him with trepidation (he was the only passenger not seasick, he reported), Tchaikovsky was somewhat put out to find no one to greet him, but felt much better after his enthusiastic reception at the concert in St James's Hall. He conducted the

evergreen Serenade and the Third Suite in G (Opus 55). The only complaint was that the concert had not included a more substantial work.

This concert marked the beginning of Tchaikovsky's enormous and unbroken popularity in Britain. As for the composer himself, he had never been an Anglophile, once remarking that Dickens and Thackeray were the only people he could forgive for being English, and his brief visit to a gloomy London in March did not do much to alter his opinion.

The English may have had some effect on him all the same, for on his way home he went to a performance of *The Mikado* in Vienna. Alas, by the end of Act I, his seat was empty.

He was hugely relieved to get back home ('All the foreign countries seem like a dream'), but the tour had been a success, and even Tchaikovsky took some satisfaction from it.

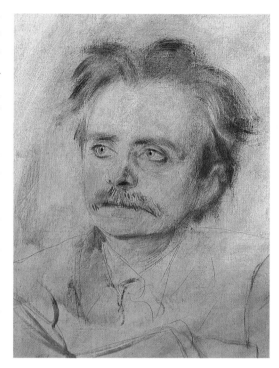

Left *Grieg, also present at Leipzig in 1888, won Tchaikovsky's full and instant approval.*

Left *In Prague Tchaikovsky's concerts became the occasion for pro-Russian demonstrations, the Czechs being favourably inclined towards their fellow Slavs but not to their Austrian rulers.*

Above *Dvorák, encountered in Prague in 1888, was also wholly sympathetic to Tchaikovsky, not least because he was so flattering.*

CREATIVE SURGE

Alexey had found another house near Klin, and by the time he arrived, in May 1888, it was all ready for him, though rather cold, to which he ascribed his catching a chill. The view was wonderful 'and what is even nicer is that you can step out of the garden right into the woods and roam there all day. No trace of any dacha inhabitants.'

What with his cold and the reaction from his travels, he was feeling run down. But he had already announced his intention of writing a symphony this summer. 'How tired I am,' he wrote to Modest, 'and how I want to work, only work, and only the knowledge of doing something positive can bring me peace and health.' In a period of just five weeks in his new house, and in spite of several days absence in Moscow on business, he completed the short score of his Fifth Symphony and also the *Hamlet* Overture (much less successful than *Romeo and Juliet*).

For some people, who find the Sixth Symphony too grim, Tchaikovsky's Fifth Symphony is a favourite work. It was a great advance on the Fourth Symphony, especially in terms of structure, for example in the way the opening theme constantly returns, running through the whole work and showing how Tchaikovsky had benefitted from his experience with the *Manfred* Symphony. Some critics have expressed doubts about the finale, but perhaps only as a result of misconceiving the composer's intentions. Contemporary critics like Cui could not make head or tail of it.

By the autumn Tchaikovsky was preparing for another international tour. In one way the prospect depressed him, but the acclaim and the cash were large compensations. The deaths of his old friend and associate, Hubert, and his niece Vera (wife of Rimsky-Korsakov) plunged him further into gloom, alleviated to some degree by preliminary work on a new ballet, *The Sleeping Beauty*, and by the company of his 'divine' nephew Bob, during a visit to St Petersburg. In Berlin the following February he was also cheered by seeing a lot of his old 'flame' Désirée Artöt, whose talent he had always admired, even after she had (according to him) grown very fat and lost her voice, while Paris was brightened by the presence of the latest young pianist to attract him, Vasily Sapelnikov (1868–1941).

Nikolay Hubert (1840–88), fellow-student and long associate of Tchaikovsky. He succeeded Nikolay Rubinstein as director of the Moscow Conservatoire.

*Tchaikovsky with
'Bob' Davidov,
about 1891.*

Brahms stayed on an extra night in Hamburg especially to hear Tchaikovsky conduct the Fifth Symphony (he said he liked all of it except the last movement; Tchaikovsky agreed). In London Sapelnikov played the First Piano Concerto with the composer conducting, to great acclaim.

London was the last stop, but Tchaikovsky returned via Constantinople and Tblisi, where Anatoly lived, to Moscow and St Petersburg, where discussions were held concerning the settings for *The Sleeping Beauty*.

The lavish production of this famous ballet took place in January 1890. The tsar attended the dress rehearsal and pronounced it 'very charming', which to Tchaikovsky seemed excessively cool. It was not a great success with the critics either. They were accustomed to ballet in which the – mediocre – music existed merely to give the stars opportunities to show off their technique. *The Sleeping Beauty* did not really come into its own until Diaghilev and Stravinsky got their hands on it nearly twenty years after Tchaikovsky's death.

Afterwards Tchaikovsky went abroad again, with the deliberate intention of writing an opera. He did not know where he wanted to go, and had already started on the journey before he decided on his final destination – Florence.

But he *did* know what the opera was going to be – *The Queen of Spades*, based on Pushkin with libretto by the composer's brother Modest. Tchaikovsky himself had

Left *A performance
of* The Sleeping
Beauty *by the Royal
Ballet in London,
1986.*

Right *The set for*
The Sleeping
Beauty *at the
Maryinski Theatre,
St Petersburg, in
January 1890.
The Tsar, to
Tchaikovsky's
disgust, merely
remarked that the
ballet was 'very
nice'.*

been mulling over the project for some time. What finally sparked off his creative enthusiasm was the interest in it shown by the directors of the Imperial Theatres when he had mentioned it to them during rehearsals for *The Sleeping Beauty*.

As so often on arriving in a foreign country, he was lonely and depressed, feeling at times weary with life itself. Even Florence was 'boring and disgusting'. But he worked like a demon. The story appealed to him, and he was easily able to identify with the ill-starred hero and heroine locked in a losing battle against 'Fate'. So thoroughly was he involved in the work, Tchaikovsky wrote, that the scene in which the Countess dies of fright also gave him the terrors.

He worked with such speed that Modest was mildly alarmed. Tchaikovsky was determined to finish the opera by the spring, which would enable it to be performed next

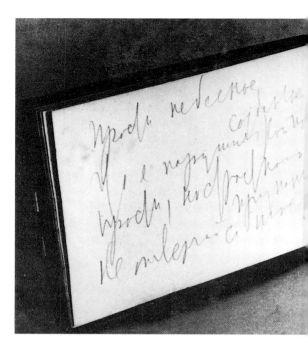

No. 24 Fontanka, St Petersburg. Modest Tchaikovsky had a flat in this building where the composer often stayed, on one occasion meeting Anton Chekov at lunch.

season, and Modest could not always keep up with him. As a result, the libretto owes much to the older brother.

AN ERA CLOSES

In the autumn of 1890 Tchaikovsky was once again staying with Anatoly's family in Tblisi, when he received a letter from Mme von Meck telling him that as a result of financial disaster she would have to discontinue the allowance she had been paying him for the last 13 years. Surprised and shocked, he wrote back saying that the money did not matter (though he still often complained of a shortage of cash, he really did not need the allowance any more) and expressing dismay at her closing words: 'Do not forget, and think of me sometimes.' As if he would forget her!

Above
Tchaikovsky usually carried a notebook such as this in which he jotted down musical ideas. The page at right contains thoughts and comments concerning The Queen of Spades, *which occupied him in 1889.*

Her friendship and support were much more important than the money.

He soon discovered that Mme von Meck's excuse for ending his annuity was pure fiction; in fact she wanted to end the relationship, and he never heard from her again.

Why? No one can say, though many reasons can be – and have been – suggested. This strange lady had always been eccentric, to say the least. Some of her letters are not those of a wholly sane person, and by this time her physical as well as her mental health was deteriorating (she outlived Tchaikovsky by only a few weeks).

Although their correspondence had been less voluminous in recent years, Tchaikovsky was deeply hurt. He felt betrayed, as though he had been given the sack like a servant, and being unaware of (or unable to appreciate) Mme von Meck's state of health, the bitterness remained with him. The two families remained on friendly terms but, according to Modest, Tchaikovsky uttered reproaches against Mme von Meck as he was dying.

One immediate, noticeable result was a temporary slowdown in Tchaikovsky's creative activity. In Kiev for a (very successful) production of *The Queen of Spades* in January 1891, he wrote to Modest: 'My head is empty and I have no wish to work.' He debated cancelling his forthcoming international tour, but as it included a visit to the United States, which he had long been anxious to visit, he finally decided to go. Having made that decision, he set to work again at his accustomed punishing pace. He wanted to get as much done as he could before he set off, and he had accepted commissions for a new opera, *Iolanta*, and a new ballet, *The Nutcracker*. He was still working on the latter on the train to Berlin, his first stop.

A production of The Queen of Spades *by the Kirov Opera, 1987.*

*The Tchaikovsky
brothers, about
1890. Left to right:
Anatoly, Nikolay,
Ippolit, the
composer, Modest.*

While he was in France en route for Le Havre, his sister Sasha died. Tchaikovsky was staying in Rouen at the time, because nobody knew him there, and the news was sent to Modest, who was in Paris. Modest at once set out for Rouen, but having arrived there, he decided not to tell his brother the sad news on the eve of his departure. As it happened, the sailing was delayed and Tchaikovsky returned to Paris for a couple of days, where he learned of Sasha's death from a newspaper. He could not very well cancel his trip at such a late stage, nor was the news, however grim, entirely unexpected, since Sasha had been ill for some time. But he boarded the ship in despondent spirit. Before they were out of the Channel, one of the passengers, a young man, committed suicide by throwing himself into the sea.

FEAR OF DECLINE

In spite of this inauspicious beginning, the American trip was a triumph. Like nearly every other European visitor, he was vastly impressed by New York and by the hospitality of the Americans (their generally awful food notwithstanding).

Of the six concerts in which he was due to take part, the most important was the first, as it was the first concert held in the newly completed Carnegie Hall. Only one work by Tchaikovsky was included, the *Coronation March* of 1883, but it was a great honour, and a mark of his international stature, to be invited to take part.

Tchaikovsky reckoned he aroused greater enthusiasm in America than he ever had anywhere else. However, because of the shortage of rehearsal time, none of his major works was played except for the ever-popular First Piano Concerto. The critics were generous in their praise, though he was a little annoyed to be described, by the *New York Herald*, as an interesting-looking man 'well on to 60', when he was in fact still only 50. Journalists ought to do a little more research no doubt, but otherwise the mistake was understandable. Tchaikovsky had aged fast; photographs of him at this time show a man who looks every day of 60.

He was aware of this. At home again he wrote to his adored nephew Bob, with whom

Carnegie Hall (at that time known as the Music Hall) in New York City, where Tchaikovsky conducted his Coronation March *at the inaugural concert in 1891.*

he was increasingly obsessed, 'The old man is definitely deteriorating. Not only is his hair getting thin and as white as snow, not only are his teeth dropping out . . . not only is his sight failing . . . not only are his legs starting to slow down – but the one faculty he possesses is beginning to fade and vanish.' This last fear was a perennial one, occasioned by his conviction that *The Nutcracker* was not as good as *Sleeping Beauty*, and that *Iolanta* lacked originality. To some

extent his judgment in both cases was accurate. Many critics would concur with Rimsky-Korsakov that *Iolanta* is 'one of Tchaikovsky's feeblest compositions'.

Another new piece, the symphonic ballad *The Voyevoda* (Opus 78; it has no connection with the early opera of the same name) also failed to please the composer. It was performed in Moscow in November, but in spite of its success with the public the orchestral players did not like it and friendly

A photograph of Tchaikovsky inscribed to Valérie, wife of Felix Mackar, with a fragment of the Andante Cantabile from his First String Quartet of 1871.

critics like Taneyev were hard-pressed to be tactful. Tchaikovsky afterwards destroyed the score, but the orchestral parts survived and the work was reconstructed after his death.

His next work was also a failure, a symphony in E flat major which was eventually abandoned (he scored the first movements as a piano concerto, Opus 75, and after his death Taneyev added *Andante* and finale from the composer's sketches).

At the end of 1891 Tchaikovsky embarked, without enthusiasm, on another tour. He had engagements booked in Poland, Germany, the Netherlands and Czechoslovakia. In Hamburg he was due to conduct a performance of *Eugene Onegin*, but discovered at rehearsals that his German was not good enough, so he vacated the podium for the resident conductor, none other than Gustav Mahler (1860–1911), previously unknown to Tchaikovsky. Tchaikovsky praised Mahler's performance highly.

From Hamburg he went to Paris, as he had a couple of weeks free before he was due to conduct in Holland. But he was longing to get back to Russia, and in particular to see Bob, so he cancelled his Dutch engagements and went home. Alexey was organizing his move to yet another house near Klin, his last, which became the Tchaikovsky Museum after his death.

Overwork on the E flat major symphony

A corner of the museum/house at Klin and (opposite) Tchaikovsky's study, preserved today much as it was in his lifetime despite serious damage suffered during the German invasion of 1941.

soon produced symptoms of nervous strain, and the doctor advised three weeks in Vichy, which Tchaikovsky had found a most unalluring place on his previous visit 16 years before. This time he was accompanied by Bob, but even Bob's presence did not make the spa attractive. The first seven days, Tchaikovsky wrote to Modest, felt like seven months. But he, and Bob, stuck it out for the recommended three weeks.

In September he was in Vienna. 'Why the hell do I accept these foreign invitations?' he wondered. 'Just boredom and torture.' The concert hall where he was supposed to conduct turned out to be 'a huge restaurant, stuffy from lack of air and the fumes of cheap oil and other cooking ingredients.' He insisted on the tables being removed, which was done, but still not satisfied, he cancelled his appearance and fled with relief to the secluded castle ('grand, heavenly, beautiful') of his friend, the pianist Sophie Menter.

Musically, Tchaikovsky seemed to have reached a nadir. The first performance of *The Nutcracker* and *Iolanta* as a double bill in December was a comparative failure, and in Berlin, where he promptly fled after the first night, Tchaikovsky came to the con-

Varvara Nikitina and Pavel Gerat in the first production of The Nutcracker *at the Maryinski Theatre, St Petersburg, in December 1892, performed as a double bill with the opera* Iolanta.

Vichy in the 1890s. In spite of the presence of 'Bob' Davidov, Tchaikovsky did not enjoy his stay at the French spa in 1892.

clusion that the E flat major symphony on which he had been working most of the autumn was no good. He was more than ever convinced that he was written out. He told Modest that he was going to compose some songs and piano pieces in order to make money, and after that just one more opera and one final symphony, to close his career.

In fact it did look for a time as though this time Tchaikovsky's fear of failing powers might be true; but having conceived another symphony, by the end of February 1893 his mind was full of it. This swiftly ended his fears: he was soon describing the new work in his letters as his greatest masterpiece. He had said that of several earlier works, only to change his mind later. But this time he was right. He was, as always, reluctant to put it aside in order to carry out other more mundane tasks, and felt compelled to finish it as quickly as possible.

GENIUS FULFILLED

The symphony was to be a 'programme symphony but with a programme which would be a mystery to everyone,' he wrote. 'You can't imagine what joy I feel now that I am convinced that my time is not over yet and that I am still able to work.'

Though interrupted by concerts in Moscow and Kharkov, he finished the short score at the end of March. He then turned to the commercial work he had mentioned to Modest before starting on the orchestration (which he always liked to mull over for a while), spending some time in Moscow during May where he attended the first performance of the 19-year-old Rachmaninov's first opera.

At the end of the month he left for England. He had been awarded an honorary doctorate of music by Cambridge University, along with Grieg, Saint-Saëns and several other notable composers. On the way he conducted his Fourth Symphony in London, 'a veritable triumph', he reported, though he still found London an unattractive city. Cambridge was better: he liked the medieval aspects and general atmosphere of the place.

Grieg unfortunately was too ill to attend, but Tchaikovsky was pleased to see Saint-Saëns, with whom he always got on well. In Moscow in 1875 they had staged an impromptu ballet together on the Pygmalion theme. Tchaikovsky played Pygmalion and Saint-Saëns played Galatea, to music improvised by Nikolay Rubinstein – an event one would like to have witnessed.

Tchaikovsky, for all his fits of extreme despondency and despair, his tortured emotional conflicts and his neurotic dislike of society, was of course perfectly capable of having a good time, as plenty of his music testifies. His horror of social occasions did not extend to parties with good friends, parties which often went on well into the small hours and included some awesome drinking. Tchaikovsky was one of those who can both eat and drink large quantities without suffering for it later. That he never

Tchaikovsky in academic robes to receive an honorary doctorate of music at Cambridge University in June 1893.

70

grew fat must have been due to his abnormal expenditure of nervous energy and perhaps also to his habit of taking long daily walks.

By the end of July he was back at Klin. Although he enjoyed his rural seclusion, he did sometimes complain of being bored in the evenings. His work came first, however, and notwithstanding his ability to compose in less than ideal surroundings, he worked better on his own at Klin than he did anywhere else.

At this time his loneliness was exacerbated by his longing for Bob Davidov. His letters to that young man had often contained rather plaintive requests for an answer and, having spent a few days in Bob's company at Modest's home after returning from England, he felt his nephew's neglect the more keenly. Why did Bob take so little interest in him? he wondered. Perhaps he would not, as he had intended, dedicate his new symphony to him (he did though).

He was finding the orchestration difficult, and it took longer than usual, though very little time judged by less superhuman standards than Tchaikovsky's. Sometimes he felt he was slowing down. Once he spent the whole day sitting over two pages. But, though slow, the work pleased him. 'I love it as I've never loved any one of my other musical progeny,', and he acknowledged that his slowness was after all due not to failing powers but to taking greater care. The orchestration was completed, in fact, in a little over three weeks.

Significant or not, it is interesting that at this time Tchaikovsky refused a request from the Grand Duke Konstantin for a requiem on the grounds that his symphony, especially the finale, was 'permeated with a similar mood'.

In September he went to Hamburg for a

Tchaikovsky's house and garden at Klin.

production of *Iolanta*, which was quite popular for a time though seldom heard now. After some enjoyable family visits he returned to Klin, where he completed the single-movement Third Piano Concerto (Opus 75), based on his abandoned E flat major symphony, and in October he was in St Petersburg for rehearsals of the Sixth Symphony.

The attitude of the orchestral players was rather cool, which made Tchaikovsky feel despondent but did not affect his confidence in the work. He thought his conducting might be to blame. There were mixed opinions about his conducting ability: he was certainly no Mahler in this respect, but no less a judge than Rimsky-Korsakov pronounced his performance excellent. The

symphony was favourably, if not ecstatically, received, and Tchaikovsky had enough experience of St Petersburg audiences not to expect any display of fervent enthusiasm.

The next morning at breakfast Tchaikovsky, who was staying with Modest, was still trying to think of a title for the symphony, which had to be sent to Jurgenson, the publisher, that day. At that moment it was still called simply 'A Programme Symphony', which Tchaikovsky thought inadequate. Modest suggested 'Tragic', which would certainly have been a good descriptive title, but Tchaikovsky did not like it. Modest then left the room for a moment and while he was out the word *pathétique* came into his head. In English, the meaning of the

The tomb of Tchaikovsky in the cemetery of the Alexander Nevsky monastery in Leningrad (formerly St Petersburg). The graves of Glinka, Borodin and Mussorgsky are close by.

word 'pathetic' has shifted a long way from the idea of pathos, but in French this is not so, hence the preservation of the French title.

Tchaikovsky liked it at once (according to Modest) and sent the score off to Jurgenson with that title. He changed his mind the next day, saying he wanted it to be called by its number only, but *Pathétique* it has remained.

He told Jurgenson he would see him in Moscow in a few days, but he never saw Jurgenson or Moscow again. Two days later he became seriously ill, and on 6 November 1893 he died.

A LAST MYSTERY

Tchaikovsky's illness was at first ascribed to the effects of a late party with friends the previous evening. At lunch-time he ate nothing, but drank a glass of water. It was later said that, although warned of the notorious danger of St Petersburg water, he had taken it straight from the tap, refusing the normal precaution of boiling it first, and that he had contracted cholera and died a few days later.

Doubts surrounded this account from the first. Many people believed Tchaikovsky's death was due to suicide, by shooting or other means. There was also talk of blackmail. Some strange incidents connected with his death fuelled the gossip. The usual precautions to prevent spread of infection in a case of death from cholera had not been taken, the composer's illness had not been reported in the press, almost no one had seen him during the last four days of his life, and so on.

However, since no further evidence was forthcoming, it was generally established that Tchaikovsky had indeed died of cholera, whether or not he had invited his death by deliberately drinking unboiled water.

Then in 1978 Alexandra Orlova, a Tchaikovsky scholar who had worked in the Tchaikovsky Museum, emigrated to the West, bringing with her a copy of a book of Tchaikovsky's letters which had been printed in 1940 but never published because it revealed aspects of Tchaikovsky's character which the Soviet authorities wished to suppress (including evidence of his powerful homosexual drive). She also brought a new account of Tchaikovsky's death.

According to this account, a member of

Tchaikovsky's desk in the Tchaikovsky Museum at Klin.

the Russian aristocracy had complained to the tsar that Tchaikovsky had seduced his nephew. The government official who dealt with the matter had, like Tchaikovsky, once attended the School of Jurisprudence, and feared the effect of the impending scandal on the reputation of the School. He therefore arranged an informal judicial hearing of distinguished former pupils of the School, including Tchaikovsky himself and a lawyer named Vladimir Gerard who is said to have been one of Tchaikovsky's earliest loves. As a result of their deliberations Tchaikovsky agreed to commit suicide, which he did (probably) by taking arsenic.

This all sounds both unnecessary and unlikely, as unlikely as anything in Tchaikovsky's operas, but it has been widely if not universally accepted. No one seems to have had any motive to invent such a story; moreover, it comes from two apparently independent sources – the widow of the official who arranged the hearing and a

member of the Davidov family (a younger brother of Bob). What does seem likely is that the fear of damaging the reputation of the School of Jurisprudence was not the main, if any, reason for Tchaikovsky's suicide. On the other hand he had spent his whole life trying to prevent the fact of his homosexuality becoming generally known. Perhaps, too, he felt that, having written his 'requiem', it was an appropriate time for him to leave a world in which he had never felt comfortable.

Twelve days after the composer's death, a concert was arranged in his memory at which the Sixth Symphony was conducted by Eduard Nápravník (1839–1915), the Czech-born conductor of the St Petersburg Opera, probably the best conductor in Russia and a long-time supporter of Tchaikovsky. The symphony had a tremendous effect, and the impression that in the finale the composer had deliberately written a last, haunting farewell was irresistible.

The conductor Eduard Nápravník (1839–1916), from a photograph of 1897 inscribed by the subject to Ludmilla Shestakova, sister of Glinka. Among other works, Nápravník wrote an opera on a subject also exploited by Tchaikovsky, Francesca da Rimini.

Above *The monument to Tchaikovsky which stands outside the Moscow Conservatoire.*

The success of the Sixth Symphony was not confined to Russia. Few works have had such a swift and powerful impact on international musical consciousness. Tchaikovsky had become in his later years as famous and successful as practically any composer had ever managed to be in his own lifetime, but in the years following his death his popularity was greater than ever. And so far as the listening public is concerned, it has never seriously declined.

Tchaikovsky left most of his possessions to Alexey Sofronov, who was able to buy the house at Klin and reverently filled it with mementoes of the composer. Four years later he sold it to 'Bob' Davidov and Modest Tchaikovsky. Both died there, Bob by suicide in 1906 (at the age of 35), Modest of cancer ten years later. Another of Tchaikovsky's brothers, Ippolit (1843–1927), who had spent most of his active life in the Russian navy, later lived there as an unofficial curator.

Above *The ormolu clock which stood on the mantelpiece of Tchaikovsky's study. The framed picture on the right is of Alexandra Davidov.*

Left *Desk, chair and score in Tchaikovsky's bedroom.*

ЩЕЛКУНЧИКЪ

Балетъ-Фээрія

въ 2хъ дѣйствіяхъ.

МУЗЫКА

П. ЧАЙКОВСКАГО.

Op. 71.

Оркестровая Партитура	(ПОЛНАЯ)	150 Руб.
Увертюра Партитура		2 „
„ „ Голоса		2 „
Изданіе для Фортепіано	(ТАНѢЕВЪ).	5 „
„ „ „ облегченное авторомъ		4 „

Собственность издателя.

Москва у П. Юргенсона.

С.-Петербургъ у I. Юргенсона. | Варшава у Г. Зенневальда.

Рига у В. Гольца и Кⁿ.

Парижъ у Ф. Макаръ и Ноёль. | Лейпцигъ у Д. Ратера.

TCHAIKOVSKY'S MUSIC

*An international best-seller – Tchaikovsky's enduring popularity:
his melodic gifts and mastery of orchestration: his greatest works
and some recent interpretations on record*

A few years ago some painstaking person (or perhaps it was a computer) worked out that of all the hours of music broadcast in England in the course of a year, the composer whose works were played most often was Tchaikovsky. This was not a great surprise. At any time since the composer's death nearly 100 years ago, Tchaikovsky would undoubtedly have come top, or very near the top, in any popularity poll.

A poll of serious music critics would probably have produced different results. It is unlikely that Tchaikovsky would have come top of anybody's list. On some lists he would not have found a place at all.

For Tchaikovsky has always been admired – loved – by audiences more than critics. The suspicion still lurks that Tchaikovsky is not altogether a 'serious' composer. Most of his music has an immediate and powerful appeal to the emotions: it is tuneful and it is passionate. Occasionally it comes dangerously near to sentimentality, and it often betrays a certain weakness of structure (though less so than some critics, misunderstanding Tchaikovsky's purposes, have believed).

Tchaikovsky's greatest gifts as a composer were his extraordinarily fertile melodic invention combined with his vivid orchestration, and his ability to express his own powerful emotions in musical terms. Perhaps the most striking characteristic of his work as a whole is its sheer variety. He was able to speak in many musical languages including, especially in his last symphonies, a language uniquely his own. Though often regarded as one of the most thoroughly Romantic composers of the late Romantic period, he could reproduce the classical elegance of the 18th century and the dynamic rhythms of Russian folksong with equal facility. Although his output was uneven, he practised in almost all the current musical genres, from grand opera to simple song, and brought to each of them an astonishing variety of expression.

Tchaikovsky is widely recognised as the greatest genius of Russian music in the 19th century. Yet he was not, in an obvious sense, the most 'Russian'. He had a formal training at the St Petersburg Conservatoire, where he imbibed the 'Western' musical tradition and technique. It was this that separated him from Balakirev and the more narrowly

Title page of
The Nutcracker, *published by Jurgenson.*

nationalistic school of Russian music which was dominant in the remarkable outburst of Russian musical genius of which Tchaikovsky was the outstanding example. But he was a thorough Russian nationalist himself, no less than Balakirev or Borodin or Rimsky-Korsakov. He was deeply absorbed in Russian culture and, like the nationalist composers, made frequent use of Russian folksong in his music.

Because his music had few 'secrets' and expressed emotions in a strong and direct way, critics have often condemned him as superficial or shallow, and this impression has been encouraged by the way in which Tchaikovsky's works have been subjected to wholesale plunder by composers of popular music, makers of television commercials, and other brigands. Even at its most impassioned, its most 'hysterical' as some would say, Tchaikovsky's music is solidly professional, based on sound study and technique. It is always worth keeping in mind that the composer whom Tchaikovsky respected above all others was Mozart.

Although he wrote many songs, piano pieces and other short works, a large part of Tchaikovsky's works are for the orchestra, and he became the greatest exponent of orchestral 'colour'. Few composers have shown more skilful deployment of their knowledge of the characteristics of each instrument. In fact, sometimes the orchestral sound seems to have been a more

Celebration of Easter in a Russian village. Tchaikovsky wrote and arranged a great number of songs, and his music was at least as popular among ordinary Russian folk as it was in the grand concert halls and opera houses of Europe.

important consideration than the actual structure of the music.

When Mahler took over from Tchaikovsky as conductor for the German première of *Eugene Onegin* in Hamburg, he did so with great enthusiasm. Tchaikovsky described him as 'longing' to conduct the first night. Mahler must have been impressed also by the Sixth Symphony, since his own Third Symphony, written less than a year later, also has, unusually, an *Adagio* finale. His symphonic use of folk-song also owes something to Tchaikovsky's example. Though Mahler's music is not like Tchaikovsky's, both had a sense of being outcasts in society (Mahler because of his Jewishness), both were unfortunate in love, and both in their late works communicated a tragic view of human existence.

A resigned or despairing finale, as adopted by Tchaikovsky in the *Pathétique* and by Mahler most notably in his Ninth Symphony, together with a propensity for sudden, shocking contrasts, became almost fashionable after 1893. Such features are notable in works by Berg, whose totally dissimilar music nevertheless shares with Tchaikovsky's a strong emotional content, and by Bartok, whose powers of melodic invention also recall Tchaikovsky.

The effect of *Eugene Onegin* on Mahler may be compared with the effect of *The Queen of Spades* on Puccini. His powerful emotional climaxes are achieved by methods similar to Tchaikovsky's.

Left *Mozart, Tchaikovsky's hero, whose music was familiar to him as a child through the orchestrion (a kind of mechanical organ). Tchaikovsky described his attitude to Mozart then as one of 'passionate worship'.*

Gustav Mahler (1860–1911), who became chief conductor of the Hamburg Opera in 1891 and took over Eugene Onegin *at short notice, though his greatest days as an operatic conductor came later, when he was director of the Vienna Court Opera.*

Critics have also remarked upon certain similarities between Tchaikovsky and Sibelius, in spite of the generally cooler emotional temperature of the Finnish composer. In particular, Tchaikovsky's wintry symphonic ballad, *The Voyevoda* (which would be unknown today if the composer had had his way) is in some ways more 'like' Sibelius than it is like other Tchaikovsky! In Sibelius's First Symphony, the element of romantic Slavism clearly derives from Tchaikovsky, in whose time Finland was part of Russia.

Some of Tchaikovsky's music was arranged in later years by Stravinsky, who was largely responsible for the version of *The Sleeping Beauty* with which we are familiar. His work on that ballet, he said, gave him 'intense pleasure'. Stravinsky had been the pupil of Rimsky-Korsakov, but he was readier to acknowledge the influence of Tchaikovsky than that of his own master, and he played an important part in restoring Tchaikovsky's musical reputation, which among critics had sunk rather low in the early 20th century.

However, the composer who is nearest to being regarded as Tchaikovsky's musical successor is probably Rakhmaninov (1873–1943), who, like Tchaikovsky, wrote operas with fine musical qualities but poor librettos which make them unsuccessful in performance. Not that direct influence is especially strong; rather, Rakhmaninov was the last of the group of great Russians of the late 19th century whose work was characterised by strong melody, colourful orchestration and a sense of sadness or resignation to fate, a group among whom Tchaikovsky is the greatest genius.

OPERA

Tchaikovsky wrote ten operas, which is enough to contradict the general assumption that he was primarily an orchestral/instrumental composer. On the contrary, despite considerable discouragement, he persisted in his operatic efforts throughout his career.

By comparison with his work in other genres, it is true that his operas have not been very successful; only two, *Eugene Onegin* and *The Queen of Spades*, are fixtures in the international operatic repertory. But a composer's operas, with some obvious exceptions, tend always to be his or her least performed works if only on simple economic grounds: it costs a lot more to produce an opera than perform a symphony.

Moreover, most of Tchaikovsky's less well-known operas, though performed comparatively rarely, contain much splendid music. The trouble generally lies in the libretto and the defective dramatic structure.

Eugene Onegin was based on Pushkin's novel-poem. The idea took some time to grip Tchaikovsky's imagination; he was nervous of tackling a Russian literary classic, and aware that the work offered few opportunities for dramatic action: he wanted to call it 'lyric scenes' rather than 'an opera'.

In Tchaikovsky's operas there is often a key scene, which he composed first. In this case it is the 'letter scene,' Act I Scene ii, in

which the heroine, Tatyana, writes a love letter to Eugene Onegin, a rich, bored, upper-class young man whom she has fallen in love with on their first meeting, through Onegin's young friend Lensky, in the opening scene. In the letter scene Tchaikovsky demonstrates wonderful sensitivity to the emotions of a young woman.

Onegin treats Tatyana's declaration coolly, explains he cannot marry her, and advises her to practise greater self-control. Later, bored and malicious, he flirts with Olga, Tatyana's sister, who is engaged to Lensky. This leads to a quarrel, and Lensky challenges Onegin to a duel. Lensky is killed by Onegin, to the latter's remorse.

Tatyana is carted off to Moscow to find a husband, in the shape of Prince Gremin, an honourable, middle-aged soldier. Two years later Onegin meets her again at a ball in St Petersburg and realises that he is in love with her after all.

Onegin in his turn writes a love letter to Tatyana, and when he receives no reply, he goes to see her. After ordering him to leave, she admits she still loves him. But she declares she must remain faithful to her husband. Onegin rushes off in despair.

Tchaikovsky, co-author of the libretto, extracted all the lyricism from Pushkin's long poem and ignored the social satire, which was inappropriate for a Romantic

The Ball Scene, from a recent production of Eugene Onegin *by the Bolshoi Opera.*

opera and far outside Tchaikovsky's range of interest. On the whole, and notably in the letter scene, Tchaikovsky followed Pushkin very closely, and in many scenes found it necessary to invent very little.

Eugene Onegin is Tchaikovsky's greatest opera, partly because of the very feature which he feared would militate against its success, its relative lack of theatricality. It is a masterpiece of characterisation. To a Western audience it does not seem especially 'Russian', not at any rate by comparison with Mussorgsky's *Boris Godunov* or even Tchaikovsky's earlier *Vakula the Smith*, the work which is often taken to mark the end of Tchaikovsky's period of high nationalism. To a Russian audience, however, *Eugene Onegin* is perhaps more profoundly Russian than the narrower, Slavophile nationalism of Mussorgsky or Rimsky-Korsakov. Stravinsky once contradicted a young friend who remarked that he could not imagine a more Russian opera than *Boris Godunov* by saying that the most Russian opera of all was *Eugene Onegin*, not only because every young Russian woman has something of Tatyana in her but also because, from beginning to end, the atmosphere is entirely Russian. Prokofiev agreed, saying that not only Tatyana but also Olga, Onegin, Lensky and Prince Gremin are authentic Russian characters.

Outstanding recordings of the complete opera are by Levine, Dresden State Opera; Ermler, Bolshoi Opera; and Solti, Royal Opera.

The Queen of Spades also benefits from Tchaikovsky's deep involvement with his characters, this time, in particular, Hermann. When he was writing the final scene, the composer said, he felt such intense pity for Hermann that he burst into tears. The fact that Hermann was to be played by a handsome tenor whom Tchaikovsky admired no doubt helped him identify with the character.

Alexander Pushkin, whose verse novel, on which the opera Eugene Onegin *was based, is rather different in spirit.*

The Queen of Spades is also based on a work by Pushkin, the libretto being by Modest Tchaikovsky, with a good deal of help from the composer.

Hermann is in love with Liza, and she with him, though she is engaged to another man. Hermann's weakness is his love of gambling, and he discovers that Liza's elderly guardian, the Countess, knows the secret of a three-card sequence that always wins. Late at night he gets into the Countess's bedroom and in his attempts to wring the secret from her he frightens her – literally – to death. Later, however, the Countess's ghost appears to him and tells him the winning sequence: three, seven, ace.

Hermann and Liza meet by the canal opposite the Winter Palace in St Petersburg. Liza comes to realize that Hermann's love of gambling is stronger than his love for her, and in despair she throws herself into the water and drowns.

In the final scene Hermann plays cards in a gambling club. He wins a lot of money with the three-seven-ace sequence, but at the third attempt, having played the three and seven correctly, he finds that the final card, instead of being the intended ace, is the Queen of Spades. The Countess has had her revenge. Hermann loses everything and kills himself with a dagger.

This is high melodrama even by the standards of the grand opera, and the conclusion of the story is quite different in Pushkin, where Hermann ends up in the madhouse endlessly muttering 'Three-seven-ace, three-seven-*Queen*!' while Liza sensibly marries a civil servant and settles down. Obviously, that would never do for Tchaikovsky.

The strength of the opera lies in the big love duet between Hermann and Liza and some beautiful arias, plus the immensely powerful scene in the Countess's bedroom,

The Kirov Opera's production of The Queen of Spades, *1987.*

Above
*Tchaikovsky with
Nikolay and
Medea Gifner, who
originated the roles
of Herman and
Lisa in* The Queen
of Spades, *1890.*

where Tchaikovsky provides some of his most dramatic musical contrasts to heighten the tension.

It also has certain weaknesses which help explain why Tchaikovsky's operatic oeuvre as a whole is not more successful. There are, for example, some very contrived theatrical effects, such as the entrance of the Empress at the end of Act II, a superfluous incident introduced merely to provide a suitable finale. There are conventional passages like the interludes in 18th-century Rococo style, which make no positive contribution to the action. Edward Garden has pointed to the use of 'that hackneyed old war-horse, the diminished seventh – by this time not quite at the end of its career as a purveyor of evil.'

A recent recording (in Russian) of the complete opera is by Ermler and the Bolshoi Opera. There is also one by Khaikin and the Bolshoi Opera.

ORCHESTRAL WORKS

Composers sometimes reserve the symphony for their most profound musical thoughts, and this is surely true of Tchaikovsky. Although his career, like most others, had its ups and downs, and the big successes (and big failures) tended to occur sporadically, it is possible to see in his symphonies a more or less steady progression, as his technique advanced with experience and his power to express his deepest emotions expanded similarly. Thus, his last symphony (No. 6) is generally acknowledged to be his finest, and it is followed in popular estimation by its immediate predecessor (No. 5). These are well-known standards of the concert hall. His early symphonies, No. 3 particularly, are heard much less often.

The genesis of the First Symphony in G minor caused a good deal of trouble – breakdown of the composer's health, initial rejection by Anton Rubinstein and The Russian Musical Society, acceptance of two movements only after revision, and finally, after further revision, performance of the complete work – with fair success, especially the *adagio*. The symphony is called 'Winter Dreams' and has some resemblance to Mendelssohn's *Hebrides* overture, though overall there is a greater debt to Schumann.

Outstanding recordings of Tchaikovsky's early symphonies are by Karajan, Berlin Philharmonic; and Jansons, Oslo Philharmonic.

Between the First and Second Symphonies Tchaikovsky wrote his fantasy overture *Romeo and Juliet*, often cited as his first real masterpiece. It is the revised version which is usually heard today.

At the heart of the piece, which captures in stark form the fierce passion and ensuing

Eduard Nápravník conducting the symphony orchestra of the Russian Music Society in St Petersburg on 18 November 1893. This performance of the Sixth Symphony, so soon after the composer's death which it seemed to foretell, rocketed the work to fame.

tragedy of Shakespeare's young lovers (doomed love was, of course, one of Tchaikovsky's favourite subjects), lies one of Tchaikovsky's most beautiful melodies, for which even the critical Balakirev declared himself eager to embrace the composer.

Among the best modern recordings are Boult, Royal Philharmonic (HMV), LP and cassette only; Bernstein, Israel Philharmonic (Deutsche Grammophon); and Davis, Boston Symphony (Philips); the original, 1869 version of the work is among the Tchaikovsky selection in a renowned set by Simon, London Symphony (Chandos).

Tchaikovsky's Second Symphony in C minor, the *Little Russian*, is one of the most charming of his major orchestral works and the one that is closest in spirit to Balakirev, Mussorgsky and the nationalist school. The first movement in particular owes a good deal to Balakirev, the brilliant finale is indebted to Glinka, and the whole work is notable for Tchaikovsky's original and endlessly resourceful use of Ukrainian folksong.

Tchaikovsky's international fame was established by the First Piano Concerto in B flat minor, played all over the Western world by Hans von Bülow. It is probably still the most popular of all Tchaikovsky's symphonic works, and certainly the most important of his works for solo instrument and orchestra. In one way this is a paradox, because in general Tchaikovsky does not seem to have been much inspired by the piano as an instrument, and he once said he disliked the piano/orchestra combination. Neither of his other two piano concertos, nor any of his considerable quantity of other piano pieces, rate among his best works.

Nor does anyone know *why* he decided, more or less out of the blue, to write a piano concerto. It is, however, a somewhat unconventional work in the relationship of piano and orchestra. Nikolay Rubinstein unfairly accused the composer of having written a 'duel' for piano and orchestra. However, it is true that the orchestra has, so to speak, many of the best tunes, and to a certain extent the piano is treated as if it were simply one of the instruments of the orchestra.

Highbrow critics sniff loftily at this work. They are suspicious, as David Brown says, of 'the frankness and force with which Tchaikovsky declares himself' and they greatly underestimate the technical achievement of the piece, especially the first movement.

Recordings of the First Piano Concerto are legion. An interpreter who has found special favour with critics is Martha Argerich, with Dutoit, Royal Philharmonic, and also with Kondrashin, Royal Symphony; other outstanding performances are by Gilels, with Mehta, New York Philharmonic; Berman, with Karajan, Berlin Philharmonic; Rubinstein, with Leinsdorf, Boston Symphony.

The Third Symphony in D major is sometimes called 'The Polish', though there is nothing particularly Polish in it. Overall, the symphony is symptomatic of the conflict between Tchaikovsky's runaway lyrical inspiration and his desire to adhere to 'correct' form – a conflict which reflects a similar one in his private life. The first movement in particular is indebted to Schumann, possibly not a good mentor for a composer anxious to advance his structural technique. The waltz, so common a feature of Tchaikovsky's music, is derived from Glinka.

The Third Symphony is probably the least successful of Tchaikovsky's symphonies, at least in terms of frequency of performance.

Tchaikovsky's Fourth Symphony in F minor was dedicated to Nadezhda von Meck: 'our symphony' he called it in his letters to her. Unusually, Tchaikovsky sketched a programme for this symphony, in which he said that the Fate motive at the beginning is the essence of the whole work, though he

Hans von Bülow conducting in Hamburg, about 1890.

was not entirely successful in carrying out this plan: the theme appears in a rather arbitrary way in the finale, which is not considered a success. The *scherzo*, on the other hand, is Tchaikovsky at his most brilliant, and altogether the symphony marked a considerable step forward both in technique and in the expression of the composer's emotional involvement.

Currently available recordings include: Jansons, Oslo Philharmonic (Chandos); Karajan, Vienna Philharmonic (Deutsche Grammophon); Maazel, Cleveland Orchestra (Telarc); Solti, Chicago Symphony (Decca).

Tchaikovsky's Violin Concerto in D major was the result of his friendship with the violinist, Kotek. It is a highly attractive work, apparently sparked off by Kotek and the composer playing through Edouard Lalo's *Symphonie espagnole* for violin and orchestra. Tchaikovsky described this work as having 'a lot of freshness, lightness, of piquant rhythms, of beautiful and excellently harmonised melodies . . . [Lalo] . . . does not strive after profundity, but he carefully avoids routine . . . and thinks more about *musical beauty* than about observing established traditions, as do the Germans.' His words could almost serve as a description of his own Violin Concerto.

The work was written very fast, though the central slow movement caused some difficulties, the original version being scrapped altogether and a new one substituted. It is a demanding work for the soloist,

which may explain why the famous violinist Leopold Auer (1845–1930) wriggled out of giving the first performance (though he played it often enough later). But although requiring some technical fireworks, the Concerto represents Tchaikovsky at his most lyrical, built on a deceptively simple scheme, with beautiful melody, especially in the slow movement.

Nearly all the internationally famous contemporary violinists have recorded Tchaikovsky's Violin Concerto, often paired with Mendelssohn's Concerto in E minor. Currently available are those by Perlman, with Ormandy, Philadelphia Orchestra; Zukerman, with Mehta, Israel Philharmonic (a live, concert recording); Kyung Wha Chung, with Dutoit, Montreal Symphony; Milstein, with Abbado, Vienna Philharmonic; Heifetz, with Reiner, Chicago Symphony (a 1957 recording); Accardo, with Davis, BBC symphony; Mutter, with Karajan, Berlin Philharmonic.

Byron's poetic drama *Manfred* was published in 1817 and has been performed very seldom – though more often than the poet wished. The central character is a kind of magician who lives alone in a castle in the Alps tortured by guilt for some unstated cause. Like Faust, he summons spirits, who offer him everything except what he most desires – oblivion. His attempts to kill himself are frustrated and he reveals to the Witch of the Alps that the sin which tortures him is his incestuous love for his sister.

A French edition of the works of Byron – a spirit congenial to Tchaikovsky's, whose underrated Manfred Symphony was based on Byron's verse drama – on a bookshelf in Tchaikovsky's house in Klin.

Descending to the Underworld, he encounters an image of his sister, who promises him death. Back in the castle, he is unable to obey an abbot's injunction to repent and defies the spirits who come to summon him. They disappear and Manfred dies.

A programme for a symphony based on this gloomy drama was drawn up by the famous critic, Vladimir Stasov (1824–1906) for Balakirev who, after Berlioz had rejected it, urged it on Tchaikovsky. At least two years passed before Tchaikovsky took up the idea, but then, as usual, he worked very fast, fired by his disturbingly close identification with Manfred – an outsider if ever there was one. The work imposed tremendous creative pressure and marked the return of powers which had been largely in abeyance for several years.

The programme of the opera is somewhat different from the drama. Nothing is made of the incestuous element (of greater interest to Byron than to Tchaikovsky), and the final scene, in which Manfred intrudes upon an Underworld bacchanal, owes little or nothing to Byron. Moreover, Tchaikovsky did not stick very closely to the programme, feeling a need to 'recreate'.

Critics have found many reasons for attacking the *Manfred* Symphony on technical grounds, but the fact is that in performance it works very well. It was Tchaikovsky's best symphony to that date (1885) and, though neglected for many years, is now considered by some the equal of the Fifth Symphony. The influence of Balakirev accounts for the comparative lack of exhibitionism, and there are also some notably Balakirevian idioms. Schumann, whose overture on the same subject was much admired by Tchaikovsky, is another influence.

A fine recording of the Manfred Symphony, especially successful in capturing its epic qualities, was made in 1982 by Muti, Philharmonia Orchestra (HMV); other versions include Haitink, Concertgebouw Orchestra (Philips), LP and cassette only.

In the spring of 1888 Tchaikovsky was admiring the flowers in his garden and idly musing on the talents he might, or might not, possess as a gardener, since musical ideas had deserted him. By midsummer, however, he had embarked on his Fifth Symphony in E minor, and was admitting that inspiration seemed to have returned. He had finished it by September and conducted the first performance in St Petersburg in November. It was not a success, and Tchaikovsky went through a characteristic spell of disillusion with the work, comparing it unfavourably with the Fourth Symphony. Both he and the public soon adopted wiser judgements of this superb symphony, Tchaikovsky's finest work so far.

A brief note, not finished, of Tchaikovsky's ideas for the symphony has survived: 'Introduction. Complete resignation before Fate or, which is the same, before the inscrutable predestination of Providence. Allegro (I) Murmurs, doubts, lamentations, reproaches against XXX. (II) Shall I throw myself into the embraces of Faith???' This does not get us very far, however. Perhaps Shostakovich summed up the Fifth Symphony as well as possible in a single sentence: 'Man, with all his joys and sufferings, is the basic concept of this work, which is lyrical from beginning to end.'

In the Fourth Symphony Tchaikovsky had spoken of the Fate theme as the essence of the whole work, but had scarcely made it so. In the Fifth Symphony he was completely successful and showed himself to be, after all, a master of the cyclic form. Not only does the memorable 'Fate' theme with which the symphony begins reappear in the other movements, it permeates the whole work. The symphony is one of the most dramatic of Tchaikovsky's works, full of sudden, exciting contrasts and vivid orchestration. Adverse criticism has been directed at the finale, on the grounds that the apparently triumphant ending seems hollow in view of what has gone before. It has also been suggested, however, that this is precisely how it is meant to sound, there being no 'triumph' over Fate.

Among modern interpreters of Tchaikovsky a high position is held by the Leningrad-trained conductor, Jansons, with the Oslo Philharmonic; another famous version is Karajan, with the Vienna Philharmonic (Karajan has recorded Tchaikovsky's late symphonies at least four times with either the Berlin or Vienna Philharmonic). Other notable versions currently available are: Kempe, Berlin Philharmonic; Previn, Royal Philharmonic; Abbado, Chicago Symphony; Muti, Philharmonia Orchestra.

The Sixth Symphony in B minor was Tchaikovsky's last major work and is, by general agreement, his finest. During his travels of 1892–93 he wrote, 'the idea of a new symphony came to me, this time having a programme, but a programme that will be a puzzle for everyone . . . the programme of this symphony is totally imbued with myself and frequently in the course of my journey I wept copiously . . . There will be a great deal that is new in the form of this work and the finale is not to be a loud *allegro* but a very slow *adagio* . . .'. In a note found after his death he described the programme: 'The essential essence of the plan of the symphony is LIFE. First movement – all impulse, passion, confidence, desire for activity. Has to be short. (Finale DEATH – result of collapse). Second movement – love; third – disappointments; fourth ends fading away (also short).' He did not follow this sketch very closely; for example, neither the first nor last movement is short, rather the contrary.

The first movement is solemn, even grim, and intensely dramatic, with a succession of savage contrasts heightening the tension: the chord which opens the *allegro vivo* section is guaranteed to rouse the sleepiest concertgoer. This section also incorporates a Russian Orthodox hymn.

The second movement is a waltz, melodic but somewhat gloomy, suggesting hidden menace. The third movement, *allegro molto vivace*, is a *scherzo* which develops into a mighty march, but again imbued with menace, suggesting that the officer leading this parade is none other than General Death himself.

Recordings by outstanding modern interpreters include those of Karajan (see under Fifth Symphony, above); Ashkenazy, Philharmonia Orchestra; Muti, Philharmonia Orchestra; Haitink, Concertgebouw Orchestra; Païta, National Philharmonic.

BALLET MUSIC

It has been said that all Tchaikovsky's music is dramatic. He loved the theatre and devoted prodigious efforts to opera, though seldom with entirely satisfactory results. As things turned out, Tchaikovsky's theatrical gifts were for ballet rather than opera.

One quality of Tchaikovsky's music is that it is 'moving' in a literal sense – it has movement. Taneyev complained that Tchaikovsky's symphonies contained too much 'dance music', and the operas also have their ballets. Tchaikovsky composed many fine dances, having a special fondness for the waltz. But he is remembered perhaps above all else, for his three ballets, *Swan Lake*, *The Sleeping Beauty* and *The Nutcracker*.

In ballet Tchaikovsky was an important innovator. Ballet as it existed in his day, and as the St Petersburg audiences expected to see it, was not a very distinguished art, at least not musically. The music existed primarily as an accompaniment to the dancing, and although both Mozart and Beethoven had composed ballet music, in general it was written to order by facile lightweight composers. Ballet was usually presented as a set of dances rather than a single, flowing work; plots were often flimsy or even nonexistent. It was a superficial but entertaining spectacle, not a drama.

Yet there was no lack of talent available. The great figure in Russian ballet in Tchaikovsky's time was Marius Petipa, one of a famous French ballet family, who had arrived in St Petersburg as a dancer in 1847 and by the early 1860s had become virtual dictator of the Russian ballet. He collaborated with Tchaikovsky, but the choreography and the dancers interested him most.

The only composer comparable with Tchaikovsky in the world of ballet in the 19th century was Délibes, whose *Sylvia* was vastly admired by Tchaikovsky (he said it was worth a hundred *Ring* cycles). Délibes' *Coppélia* was performed, and *Sylvia* was written though not yet produced, before Tchaikovsky wrote *Swan Lake*, but he knew nothing of either at the time. Were that no so, it would undoubtedly be said that Délibes influenced Tchaikovsky. The French ballet was, at this time, a long way ahead of the Russian, so that Délibes enjoyed some advantages that Tchaikovsky did not. Tchaikovsky said he wrote *Swan Lake* as 'a complete novice'. That was an exaggeration no doubt, but what mattered was that 'as a composer of ballets he had ideal musical equipment and remarkable natural instinct' (David Brown).

Swan Lake was commissioned, for a fee of 800 roubles, by the Imperial Theatres in Moscow, where rather more substantial ballets were acceptable than those which found favour in St Petersburg. Tchaikovsky's sources for the story are a mystery. It has even been suggested that he made up the plot himself, and he had certainly written a children's ballet for his Davidov nephews and nieces three years earlier which was called *Swan Lake*. The connection between the two is unknown, however. The full ballet was written sporadically, in intervals between other works, and does not seem to have caused any of the nervous stress and strain that accompanied most of Tchaikovsky's major compositions. It was finished by the spring of 1876 but not performed (at the Bolshoi in Moscow) until nearly a year later.

The production was by all accounts quite dreadful. There were three designers – one for each act, all equally bad – and a choreographer who was even worse. Some of Tchaikovsky's music was dropped because it was allegedly too difficult to dance to, and replaced by other dances by other composers. Nevertheless, it was fairly popular and remained in the repertory until the scenery fell to pieces in 1883, by which time about one-third of the music was by other hands than Tchaikovsky's (though the plot was still closer to his than it is in modern versions).

The critics had little notion of what Tchaikovsky was trying to do, to judge from their pig-headed reviews, but Tchaikovsky himself was less upset than usual since his heart was not really in *Swan Lake*. A substantial amount of his music was also second-hand, having been lifted mainly from his failed operas, *The Voyevoda* and *Undine*.

The ballet was not produced again until 1895, after Tchaikovsky's death. This was a new version prepared by Petipa and his assistant at St Petersburg, Mikhail Ivanov. The libretto was revised by Modest Tchaikovsky, who must have gravely offended his brother's shade by changing the originally tragic ending to a happy one. Many of the dances were savagely cut; music from elsewhere, though by Tchaikovsky at least, was introduced, and the order of the dances was changed. Nevertheless, it was this production which marked the beginning of *Swan Lake*'s great popularity.

There are many recordings of selections from *Swan Lake*. The first complete version on CD was Ozawa, Boston Symphony; Previn, London Symphony, is also a notable recording.

The Sleeping Beauty is regarded as Tchaikovsky's masterpiece of ballet – in spite of the lyrical beauty of *Swan Lake*.

Below *The Bolshoi Theatre, Moscow.*

Right *The Royal Ballet performs* The Nutcracker, *London 1985.*

Left *Natalia Bessmertnova in the Bolshoi's production of* Swan Lake.

Written in 1888–89, it originated in a suggestion by Ivan Vsevolozhsky, director of the Imperial Theatres in Moscow, and was based on Perrault's 17th-century version of the ancient fairy story. It was first performed in January, 1890, with splendid choreography by Petipa and a lavish production said to have cost 80,000 roubles.

All the same, it was not a critical success; there were complaints that it gave insufficient opportunities to the dancers and that it was too much like a symphony (a change, at least, from the criticism of the symphonies as being too much like ballet).

A better authority is Stravinsky, who later recognised *The Sleeping Beauty* as marking the establishment of ballet as a serious art form rather than a mere spectacle. For the 1910 Paris revival Stravinsky was hired by Diaghilev to orchestrate certain numbers which had not been included in the original production, and it is easy to see how sympathetic the two composers were. Some of Tchaikovsky's music in *The Sleeping Beauty* might in fact have been written by the early Stravinsky.

In Diaghilev's production, incidentally, Carlotta Brianza, the original Aurora of 1892, played Carabosse, the evil fairy. Sergeyev produced a new version for the Kirov Ballet in Leningrad in 1952, and among modern choreographers of *The Sleeping Beauty* are Nureyev, for the National Ballet of Canada in 1972 and MacMillan for the Royal Ballet in 1973.

It was an advantage that the Sleeping Beauty legend provided a strong plot, at any rate until the wedding celebrations which make up the last act, and Tchaikovsky's music is powerfully atmospheric, perfectly designed for the courtly goings-on of Act I and no less so for the forest setting of Act II, while his musical characterisation of the individual fairies in the Prologue and of the various fairy-tale characters brought on as wedding guests in the last act is vividly distinctive.

Outstanding recordings of *The Sleeping Beauty* suite are by Rostropovich, Berlin Philharmonic; Muti, Philadelphia Orchestra; Karajan, Philharmonia Orchestra; Ansermet, Suisse Romande Orchestra (an inexpensive selection of highlights from a 1959 recording of the complete set).

The Nutcracker, based on a Christmas story by E.T.A. Hoffmann, *The Nutcracker and the Mouse King*, was one of Tchaikovsky's last compositions, completed in 1892,

although he had been thinking about it for some ten years before that. What set him to work was the request for a ballet to be performed in a double bill in the 1891–92 season with a one-act opera (*Iolanta*).

The *Suite*, in which form the music is most familiar today, was already well known and extremely popular by the time the full ballet was produced in St Petersburg in December 1892, with choreography by Petipa's assistant Ivanov (Petipa himself being unwell). The critics did not like the ballet much and complained, not without some justice, that it was too long.

Tchaikovsky was never very enthusiastic about the work, and wrote to his nephew that he considered it far inferior to *The Sleeping Beauty*. Most critics would agree

with that judgment. As Edward Garden put it, 'the wedding-cake charm of *Nutcracker* has a defect for which it is impossible to excuse Tchaikovsky – it is bogus. The icing is made from saccharine and the cake itself from *ersatz* ingredients.

Ersatz or not, the charm is considerable, and the ballet contains some brilliant things, notably the famous 'Dance of the Sugar Plum Fairy', which employs the tones of the celesta, an instrument Tchaikovsky had imported from Paris at some expense. Not even in *The Sleeping Beauty* was Tchaikovsky's ability to enter a child's world of fairy tale and fantasy more brilliantly deployed.

New versions of the ballet were introduced by the Kirov in Leningrad in 1934 and the Bolshoi in 1966. Other notable choreographers of *The Nutcracker* are Balanchine for the New York City Ballet, 1954, probably the fullest version of Tchaikovsky's work; Cranko, Stuttgart, in 1966; and Nureyev for the Swedish Ballet in 1967.

The outstanding recording of the complete ballet is by Previn, London Symphony; an inexpensive version is by Schermerhorn, National Philharmonic. Among the best recordings of the *Nutcracker Suite* are Williams, Boston Pops; Karajan, Berlin Philharmonic, backed by *Romeo and Juliet*; Dorati, Concertgebouw Orchestra; Maazel, Cleveland Orchestra; Slatkin, Minnesota Symphony, backed by *Swan Lake* excerpts.

The Maryinski Theatre in Leningrad.

INDEX

PICTURE ACKNOWLEDGMENTS

Dominic Photography, Catherine Ashmore 34–35, 58–59, 62–63, 82–83, Zoë Dominic 91; E T Archive 54, 55 50-, 55 bottom right; Mary Evans Picture Library 8 top, 10–11, 19 top, 23, 24–25, 26, 30, 52 top, 52 bottom, 79 bottom, 86–87; Robert Harding Picture Library 2, 29, 47 top; Robert Harding Picture Library, Bibliothèque Nationale 21, 65, 77, Victor Kennett Collection 18–19, 43 bottom, 51 top, 59, George Rainbird 11 top, 32, 33 bottom, 38, 60, H. Roger-Viollet, SAN Viollet 72; Hutton-Deutsch Collection/Bettmann Archive 64; Larousse 60–61, 61; Mansell Collection 28, 40, 53 top, John Massey-Stewart 79 top; Novosti Press Agency 7 top, 7 bottom left, 8 bottom, 9, 12, 13, 14–15, 16–17, 19 bottom, 20, 22, 25, 31, 33 top, 36, 37, 41, 42, 43 top, 44, 45, 46, 47 bottom, 48, 49, 50–51, 53 bottom, 56, 57, 63, 66 left, 66–67, 68–69 bottom, 70, 70–71, 73, 74 right, 75 top, 75 bottom, 76, 78–79, 80–81, 82 left, 84 top, 87, 90, 90–91, 92–93; H. Roger-Viollet 7 bottom right, ND-Viollet 68–69 top; Society for Cultural Relations with the USSR 17, 74 left, 84–85; Swiss National Tourist Office/Villiger 39; ZEFA Picture Library (UK), L. Sitensky 54–55, Tom 27.